MATTRESS MONEY?!

THE STEP-BY-STEP PROVEN SYSTEM AND ACTION GUIDE FOR EARNING A 6-FIGURE INCOME WHILE WORKING YOUR SCHEDULE & SELLING MATTRESSES

DARREN BRETT CONRAD

FEATURING EXPERT BONUS CONTENT FROM OKLAHOMA'S SBA YOUNG ENTREPRENEUR OF THE YEAR,

CLAY CLARK

Mattress Money

Copyright © 2026 Clay Clark Publishing

CONTENTS

FOREWORD

I first met Darren Conrad at one of the quarterly ThrivetimeShow.com Business Growth Conferences that I was hosting at the ThrivetimeShow.com world headquarters in Tulsa, Oklahoma. I noticed Darren sitting in the front row, eagerly taking notes and mentally engaging with every speaker and every attendee in a way that is not normal. Darren was MENTALLY PRESENT AND PHYSICALLY PRESENT (which is rare to see on the planet Earth). I could tell that Darren was truly listening, absorbing and thinking intensely about how he could apply the best-practice systems and processes that I teach at my conferences to his own business. As I watched Darren engage with the content in a profound way, I didn't know that Darren had successfully opened 1,000+ mattress store locations throughout his career, I just knew that he had successfully done something. Shortly after the conference, Darren and I spoke, and it was only then that I discovered that Darren had already achieved massive success throughout his career as leader in the mattress marketplace. Having spoken at thousands of events over the past 25 years, I have found that successful people are typically pretty easy to spot in a crowd. They arrive early to everything, they aggressively take notes and they mentally participate in the constant activity of attempting to apply what they are learning.

"A Carnegie or a Rockefeller or a James J. Hill or a Marshall Field accumulates a fortune through the application of the same principles available to all of us, but we envy them and their wealth without ever thinking of studying their philosophy and applying it to ourselves. We look at a successful person in the hour of their triumph and wonder how they did it, but we overlook the importance of analyzing their methods and we forget the price they had to pay in the careful and well-organized preparation that had to be made before they could reap the fruits of their efforts."

NAPOLEON HILL

(Best-selling author of Think & Grow Rich. I named my son Aubrey Napoleon-Hill Clark after Napoleon Hill because his books and writing have forever changed my life.)

Having helped hundreds of entrepreneurs to achieve success in the world of business, I have found that many people want to become self-employed; however, they often struggle to find a business model that they can afford to start and that they have the skills and financial capacity needed to actually run successfully. As an example, if you wanted to open up a McDonald's franchise, it would now cost you over $2 million to open one (The total cost to open a McDonald's franchise business ranges between $1.4 million and $2.7 million). Think about that for a second. The costs associated with opening up a McDonald's include: the one-time franchise fee, which is $45,000, plus it requires massive investments in real estate, marketing materials, equipment, signage, staffing, landscaping and decor. Additionally, if you want to qualify to open a McDonald's franchise, you are required to have at least $500,000 in non-borrowed personal resources and must pay ongoing royalty fees.

As other examples of great business models that are simply unaffordable for most Americans:

» Sports Clips - A Sports Clips franchise ranges between $266,000 and $439,000 to open.

» Subway - A Subway franchise ranges between $100,000 to over $500,000 to open.

Within the pages of this book, Darren will teach you to affordably open and operate a successful mattress business. In full disclosure, I have never opened up a mattress business with Darren. I can tell that Darren has an electric passion to help entrepreneurs create both time and financial freedom. In this book, Darren gives you a look behind the curtain and looks into the nitty-gritty details of what it takes to start and run a successful mattress business. Although nothing in life is guaranteed, Darren appears to have nailed down a turn-key plan for starting and growing a successful mattress business. I would encourage you to read this book with a healthy dose of skepticism and paranoia. Additionally, I would highly recommend that you ask Darren any questions that you have about the business model and the action steps that it takes to successfully run a thriving and profitable mattress business.

How does America Bedding Direct work?

BEHOLD!
THE AMERICA BEDDING DIRECT WORKFLOW

AMERICA
BEDDINGDIRECT

WORKFLOW

MARKETING

GOOGLE LOCAL REVIEWS ★★★★

SEO

FACEBOOK ADVERTISING
- BOOSTED ADS
- MARKETPLACE
- JOIN GROUPS

SIGNAGE & PRINT
- ROAD SIGNS
- FLIERS
- BUSINESS CARDS

4-LEGGED MARKETING STOOL

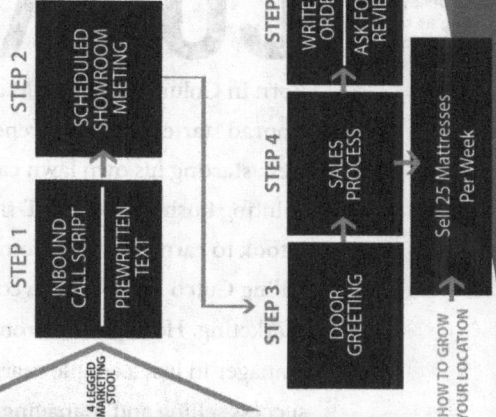

STEP 1 — INBOUND CALL SCRIPT / PREWRITTEN TEXT

STEP 2 — SCHEDULED SHOWROOM MEETING

STEP 3 — DOOR GREETING

STEP 4 — SALES PROCESS

STEP 5 — WRITE UP ORDER / ASK FOR A REVIEW

STEP 6 — DAILY TRACKING

STEP 7 — ON-GOING TRAINING

HOW TO GROW YOUR LOCATION

Sell 25 Mattresses Per Week

SYSTEMS TO MASTER:

1 ADS
2 PHONE SCRIPT
3 DOOR GREETING
4 SALES PROCESS
5 B.O.M.
6 DAILY TRACKING
7 ON-GOING TRAINING

WHO IS DARREN CONRAD?

Born in Columbus, Ohio, March 24, 1970, Darren Conrad started his entrepreneurial spirit as a young teen, starting his own lawn care business, house painting business, selling T-shirts, and doing whatever it took to earn his own income. At 19, he started selling Cutco knives with a company called Vector Marketing. He advanced from sales rep to district manager in just a couple years. After having national success selling and managing Cutco Offices, he closed his doors and went to Ohio State where he graduated with a bachelor of science in consumer affairs in 1998. For the past 25 years, Darren Conrad has been building multiple successful national mattress companies with a unique retail business model to teach people how to ignite their own entrepreneur spirit. Darren teaches entrepreneurs how to run a successful business and earn an incredible profit, while having time with your friends and family. In 2020, Darren had a supernatural encounter with God, which changed his life in an amazing way. Darren has a podcast called "Get on the Ark" where he shares testimonies of how people met Jesus and how it has changed their lives just like it changed his. His passion is his family, his friends and fishing. Darren has a fishing team and its name is God's Reel.

WHO IS CLAY CLARK?

Welcome to the start of your success story. Discipline is the bridge between dreams and accomplishment. Remember it's hard to build a reputation based on what you intend to do. Let's go dominate and get stuff done.

Clay Clark

I'm Thom Clark's son. I miss you Dad.

My father died after a long battle with ALS in 2016.

Clay is the former U.S. SBA Entrepreneur of the Year, Co-Host of the ThriveTimeShow.com Radio Show, and the founder of ThriveTimeShow.com. Over the course of his career, he has been a founding team member of many successful companies including DJConnection.com, EITRLounge.com, MakeYourLifeEpic.com, ThriveTimeShow.com, and EpicPhotos.com (Dallas, Oklahoma City, etc.). He and his companies have been featured in Forbes, Fast Company, Entrepreneur, PandoDaily, Bloomberg TV, Bloomberg Radio, the Entrepreneur On Fire Podcast, the So Money Podcast with Farnoosh Torabi, and on countless media outlets. He's been the speaker of choice for Hewlett-Packard, Maytag University, O'Reilly Auto Parts, Valspar Paint, Farmers Insurance, and many other companies. He is the father of five kids and he is the proud owner of 40 chickens, six ducks, four cats, and Thousands of trees. Clay is an obsessive New England Patriots fan and Tim Tebow apologist. He wears a basketball jersey every day. When not chasing his kids and wife around, he enjoys reading business case studies and autobiographies about successful entrepreneurs while burning pinion wood.

February 21, 2007

Mr. Clayton Thomas Clark
DJ Connection Tulsa, Inc.
8900 South Lynn Lane Road
Broken Arrow, Oklahoma 74102

Dear Mr. Clark:

Congratulations! You have been selected as the **2007 Oklahoma SBA Young Entrepreneur of the Year**. On behalf of the U.S. Small Business Administration (SBA), I wish to express our appreciation for your support of small business and for your contributions to the economy of this State.

In recognition of your achievement, **an awards luncheon will be held Tuesday, May 22, 2007** at Rose State College in Midwest City, Okla. The luncheon is sponsored by the Oklahoma Small Business Development Center. Two complimentary luncheon tickets have been reserved for you and one guest.

Arrangements for the luncheon are still being finalized. You will be notified of the details as soon as they become available. You are encouraged to bring family, friends, and business associates. Upon presentation of your award, you will have the opportunity to make acceptance comments.

Also, for our awards brochure, please email an electronic photo of yourself to darla.booker@sba.gov by Friday, March 16.

Again, congratulations on your outstanding accomplishment.

Sincerely,

Dorothy (Dottie) A. Overal
Oklahoma District Director

66

Success is a choice. A choice to make trade-offs... a choice to get up early... a choice to skip lunch to hit a deadline... a choice to push through fear... a choice to work on the weekend to get ahead... a choice to turn off the TV and open a book... a choice to hold yourself and others accountable... success is a choice that I make every day.

CLAY CLARK
Founder of ThriveTimeShow.com, former U.S. SBA Entrepreneur of the Year, host of the ThriveTime Show, and America's #1 Business Coach

The F6 Life
DESIGN THE LIFE YOU WANT OR LIVE THE LIFE YOU DON'T WANT BY DEFAULT.

Psalm 118:24

"This is the day that the Lord has made. We will rejoice and be glad in it."

"Control your destiny or someone else will."

JACK WELCH
Former CEO of GE who grew the company by 4,000% during his tenure as CEW

F6

What are Your F6 Goals?

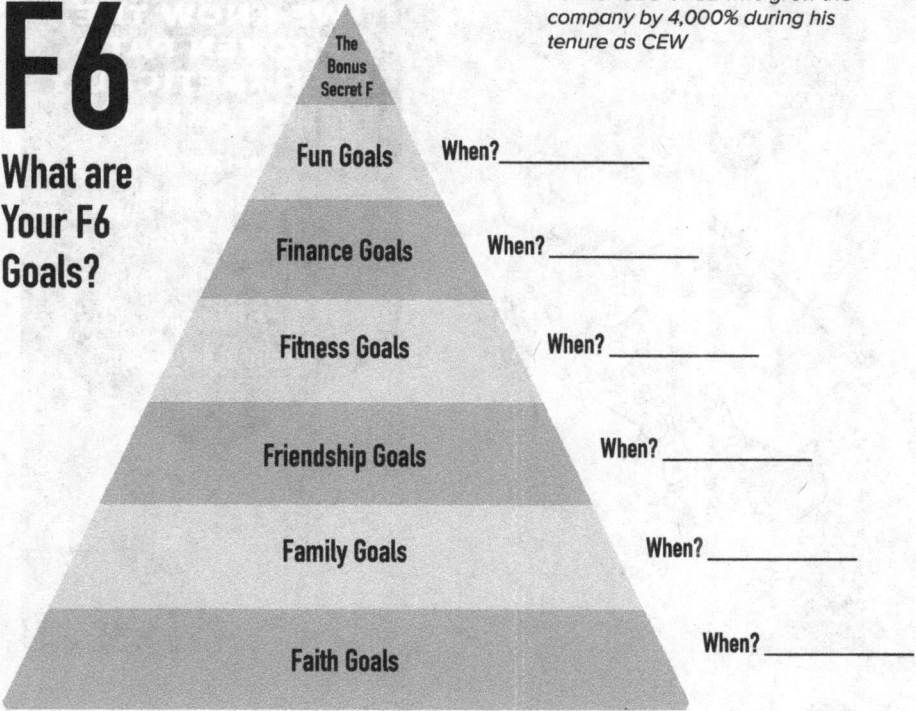

The Bonus Secret F

Fun Goals — When?_____

Finance Goals — When?_____

Fitness Goals — When?_____

Friendship Goals — When?_____

Family Goals — When?_____

Faith Goals — When?_____

What is your biggest limiting factor?

_____

What questions do you have?

_____

BE COACHABLE

WE KNOW THE PROVEN PATH

> "Nothing is as powerful as a changed mind."

TD JAKES
Bestselling author and pastor of the Potter's House.

Storytime:

The Stress of life before GPS and the consequences of not knowing where you are going

What is your biggest limiting factor?

> "One of the main reasons people don't improve is that they are not honest with themselves."

LEE COCKERELL

Thrive15.com mentor and investor and the former Executive Vice President of Operations for the Walt Disney World Resort. As the Senior Operating Executive for ten years, Lee led a team of 40,000 Cast Members and was responsible for the operations of 20 resort hotels, 4 theme parks, 2 water parks, a shopping and entertainment village and the ESPN sports and recreation complex.

Having personally grown dozens of successful businesses, I know the importance of being coachable. Having been invited to speak or consult with America's largest and most successful companies including Maytag University, O'Reilly's Auto Parts, Hewlett Packard, Valspar Paint, Chevron, UPS, etc...I have witnessed firsthand how thirsty for knowledge and coachable the top business leaders are. Having personally spoken to and coached hundreds of clients and thousands of workshop / conference attendees on how to grow a successful business **I NEED TO CHALLENGE YOU HERE TO BECOME COACHABLE.**

I NEED TO CHALLENGE YOU HERE. I NEED TO CHALLENGE YOU TO COMMIT TO NOT LETTING YOUR OWN EMOTIONS, THE EMOTIONS OF OTHERS, AND EXCUSES YOU MAKE FOR YOURSELF TO CAUSE YOU TO DANGEROUSLY DRIFT AND TO NEGATIVELY TRANSFORM YOU INTO BECOMING BOTH UNCOACHABLE AND PIG-HEADED IN YOUR WRONGNESS THAT HAS RESULTED IN YOU CONSISTENTLY BEING UNABLE TO PRODUCE THE RESULTS THAT YOU SEEK. If you do a quick Google search, you will quickly discover that Forbes reports eight out of ten businesses fail. From my first-hand experience, I believe that 8 out of 10 business owners fail because they are uncoachable. However, I can empathize with what it is like to be uncoachable because I was once uncoachable too. And I suffered because of it.

> "Most real failures are due to limitations which men set up in their own minds."
>
> **NAPOLEON HILL**
> *The author of the number one best-selling self-help author of all time, Think and Grow Rich, and the man whom my son is named after Aubrey Napoleon-Hill Clark*

Before I had mentors like David Robinson, Doctor Zoellner, Lee Cockerell, and Clifton Taulbert in my life, I was a "happy hoper" and not a "diligent doer." I once falsely believed that my own lack of success was the result of losing the genetic lottery. I used to believe I could not raise the capital I needed to grow my business because of my lack of luck and the fact that I grew up without money. I used to believe that my lack of sales results were based upon my unchangeable "God-given personality." While building my first business, I used to lazily believe that my lack of leads were the result of not "having enough word of mouth," which is impossible to generate if you don't have any customers yet.

> "Ninety-nine percent of the failures come from people who have the habit of making excuses."
>
> **GEORGE WASHINGTON CARVER**
> *A famous American botanist and inventor whose birthday was unknown because he was born into slavery in Missouri. What excuses could he have made for himself?*

> "To me job titles don't matter. Everyone is in sales. It's the only way we stay in business."
>
> **HARVEY MACKEY**
> *Best selling author and award winning entrepreneur*

I used to falsely and ignorantly (I did not know better) believe that my website's rank in Google was one of those things I could not control. I used to believe that my chronic lateness was due to the weather, the traffic, or something I ate the night before. I used to believe my lack of success was all justifiable and not something that I could ever control. Because most people are not successful, they patted me on the back and said the following poverty creating and justifying statements to me:

🛒 POVERTY CREATING MINDSETS AND JUSTIFICATION STATEMENTS:

1. "You don't need to give that speech. I know you've always struggled with stammering and stuttering."

2. "Hey, you overslept, don't worry about it. Maybe you are just not a morning person."

3. "Well, maybe it's just not meant to be."

4. "It takes money to make money."

5. "Stop striving so hard and focus on what really matters."

6. "Your sales are down because the company's culture isn't right... it's just too hard to manage millennials..."

7. "Maybe managing people, dealing with confrontation, and managing the numbers is just not your thing."

8. "Don't feel bad. You probably just don't have time to read all of that stuff right now...you have so much going on in your life with the upcoming wedding and all..."

9. "Don't sweat it...I know I couldn't focus on running a business if my best friend was suddenly killed in a car accident either."

10. "Hey, maybe you shouldn't do a radio show this year. I know that I personally couldn't focus on writing outlines if I knew my Dad was dying from ALS (Lou Gehrig's Disease) either."

11. "Once you hit your financial goals, you need to sit down and really plan out what you want to do with the rest of your life."

12. "It's too late for you to do that with your career. You need to be realistic."

13. "You really can't go around saying that stuff or you are going to irritate half of your potential customers."

And then, when I finally was able to get in-person coaching from millionaires, mentors, and real-life entrepreneurs who had been able to turn their dreams into reality, I was told uncomfortable wealth-creating and excuse-destroying statements like:

$ WEALTH CREATING MINDSETS AND PERSONAL ACCOUNTABILITY STATEMENTS:

1. "You can either get bitter or better. The choice is yours."
   Clifton Taulbert (*An African American man who was not allowed to go into banks as a kid due to legal segregation and who went on to start his own bank*)

2. "With self-discipline almost anything can be achieved in every aspect of life."
   Lee Cockerell (*Thrive15.com investor, author, and the former Executive Vice President of Walt Disney World Resorts who never fails to deliver tough love when needed*)

3. "When you do hard things life gets easier."
   Lee Cockerell (*A man who diligently worked his way up from the bottom of the Marriott Hotels payroll to being the head of Walt Disney World Resorts and being responsible for managing 40,000 team members*)

4. "If you can't delay gratification, save money, and build your war chest, then you will lose."
Doctor Robert Zoellner *(The man who started out washing dishes at a Mexican restaurant and who has now built the region's most successful auto auction, optometry clinic, horse-breeding facility, and numerous other successful small businesses)*

5. "You either pay now or pay later with just about every decision you make about where and how you spend your time."
Lee Cockerell *(Thrive15.com investor and the man who once drove to a speaking event while wearing a colostomy bag after surgery so that he wouldn't miss his speaking event)*

6. "Whatever you accept is what you should expect."
Doctor Robert Zoellner *(The closest thing I have to a living father, the Thrive15.com CEO, and the optometrist-turned Tulsa business tycoon who now co-hosts the ThriveTime Show with me every day for two hours of power. You can listen to all of the archived podcasts at ThriveTimeShow. com)*

7. "One way to get your priorities accomplished is to schedule them into your calendar."
Lee Cockerell *(The former Executive Vice President of Walt Disney World Resorts)*

8. "Rich people have big libraries, poor people have big TVs."
Doctor Robert Zoellner *(The Thrive15.com CEO, and the optometrist-turned Tulsa business tycoon who now co-hosts the ThriveTime Show with me every day for two hours of power. You can listen to all of the archived podcasts at ThriveTimeShow.com)*

9. "I know this is tough buddy, but you have to stay focused and deliver. Your Dad is going to die a slow and painful death unless God works a miracle. Call me and we'll MAN-CAVE it this weekend."
Doctor Robert Zoellner *(My business partner and the man who is the closest thing I have to a living father)*

10. "Your customers hold you to a high standard. If you want to achieve true excellence, raise that bar even higher for yourself, your colleagues, and everyone around you."

Lee Cockerell *(The former Executive Vice President of Walt Disney World Resorts who once was responsible for managing over 40,000 humans. Could you even imagine that?)*

11. "Your happiness comes from designing and living the life you want right now. When are you going to lose that suit?"

Doctor Robert Zoellner *(A man who began wearing soccer jerseys and casual clothes every day as soon he was able to build a business system that was capable of producing revenue for him when he was not personally seeing patients)*

12. "The quality of your life is directly affected by how and where you spend your time."

Lee Cockerell *(The former Executive Vice President of Walt Disney World Resorts who once built the systems needed to help him manage Walt Disney World Resorts and the nearly one million customers (guests) that visit their theme parks each week)*

13. "You need to focus on providing business school without the bs to entrepreneurs and wantrepreneurs in a real, raw, and unfiltered way like you always have."

Doctor Robert Zoellner *(A man who routinely uses that side of his massive optometry clinic located next to Oklahoma's most bustling mall to promote his political candidate of choice without worrying about the 50% of people that his pro-capitalist candidates may often upset)*

Everybody Needs a Coach

"

"The advice that sticks out I got from John Doerr, who in 2001 said, "My advice to you is to have a coach." The coach he said I should have is Bill Campbell. I initially resented the advice because, after all, I was a CEO. I was pretty experienced. Why would I need a coach? Am I doing something wrong? My argument was, "How could a coach advise me if I'm the best person in the world at this?" But that's not what a coach does. The coach doesn't have to play the sport as well as you do. They have to watch you and get you to be your best. In the business context, a coach is not a repetitious coach. A coach is somebody who looks at something with another set of eyes, describes it to you in [his] words, and discusses how to approach the problem."

ERIC SCHMIDT
The CEO and Chairman of Google in FORTUNE Magazine

THE GROWTH-FOCUSED MINDSET OF A SUCCESSFUL ENTREPRENEUR

Every day you invest 1 to 2 hours planning out your day, organizing your life, and self-examining where you are and where you want to be in the areas of Faith, Family, Friendships, Fitness, Fun, and Finances. YOU ARE COACHABLE when it comes to learning and executing the proven routines, strategies, systems, and habits of successful people. You are intentional every day about designing and living the life you want to live. You feel in control of where you are going because although life may have given you difficult circumstances, you know that you are in control of how you choose to respond to them. You understand and embrace that strength comes as a result of struggle. You understand and embrace the exponentially compounding power of scheduling daily diligence into your life. You know how to consistently apply effort, even on the days when you don't feel like it. You recognize that it is up to you to seek out wise counsel from mentors who know the proven path to speed up the achievement of your success and to avoid running over the landmines that have already been well-marked by those who have gone before you. You are on time all the time and typically 15 minutes early. You rule your emotions and are not ruled by them. YOU, MY FRIEND, ARE COACHABLE.

66

> "A Carnegie or a Rockefeller or a James J. Hill or a Marshall Field accumulates a fortune through the application of the same principles available to all of us, but we envy them and their wealth without ever thinking of studying their philosophy and applying it to ourselves. We look at a successful person in the hour of their triumph and wonder how they did it, but we overlook the importance of analyzing their methods and we forget the price they had to pay in the careful and well-organized preparation that had to be made before they could reap the fruits of their efforts."

NAPOLEON HILL
The best-selling author of Think & Grow Rich, the personal apprentice of Andrew Carnegie, and the personal mentor of Oral Roberts

Dysfunctional Mindsets

PREDICTABLE, PROBLEMATIC, AND CORRECTABLE PEOPLE PATTERNS OF THE UNCOACHABLE ENTREPRENEUR:

> Circle which dysfunctional mindset best describes your former self or YOU if you are not intentional about being personally coachable and accountable.

DYSFUNCTIONAL MINDSET #1
THE EMPLOYEE-MINDSET ENTREPRENEUR

You want to be a successful entrepreneur, but you desperately want to be told that you can keep the same schedule that you had when you were a 9 to 5 employee because "you value life balance." Just like when you worked for someone else, anytime that there is snow on the road, you want to "call in and request off for safety reasons" for your own business. You want to take the day off before every major holiday and the day after every after major holiday and you are even tempted to take off those quasi-holidays that all B-level employees like (Columbus Day, etc.).

You desperately want the law of sowing and reaping not to apply during the massive amounts of days that you take off and you want to be told that once you learn the "success secrets" you are going to have a hall pass through life and that the law of cause and effect will no longer impact the results that you see in your life. My friend, this can absolutely be the year that you will achieve the success that you desire, however, you must be willing to make changes.

According to an article published by Business Insider called, *Check Out How Much the Average American Works Each Year Compared to the French, the Germans and The Koreans* the average American is now working approximately 1,680 hours per year, which, if you are dividing that by 40 hours per week, means that the average American only works 42 weeks per year.

If you take off for your birthday, your spouse's birthday, your anniversary, the days before and after each national holiday, two weeks for vacation, and when you don't feel good while starting or growing a business (before you make your millions), you will be poor.

Circle the days you took off this past year from sowing seeds, and determine how realistic it is for you to plan on reaping a harvest this year.

The day before New Year's Eve.

New Year's Eve.

New Year's Day.

The day after New Year's Day.

The day before Martin Luther King, Jr. Day

Martin Luther King, Jr. Day

The day after Martin Luther King, Jr. Day

The day before President's Day

President's Day

The day after President's Day

The Thursday before Good Friday

Good Friday

The Saturday before Easter

Easter

The day after Easter

The day before Memorial Day

Memorial Day

The day after Memorial Day

The day before Independence Day

Independence Day

The day after Independence Day

The day before Labor Day

Labor Day

The day after Labor Day

The day before Columbus Day

Columbus Day

The day after Columbus Day

The day before Veterans' Day

Veterans' Day

The day after Veterans' Day

The Monday of the week of Thanksgiving

The Tuesday of the week of Thanksgiving

The Wednesday of the week of Thanksgiving

Thanksgiving

Black Friday

The day before Christmas Eve (Known as Festivus for all of your Seinfeld fans)

Christmas Eve

Christmas Day

The day after Christmas

7 days that you don't feel like coming in because you feel sick

104 weekend days off

"

"You can't get much done in life if you only work on the days when you feel good."

JERRY WEST
Hall of Fame basketball player and legendary NBA executive

"Lazy hands make for poverty, but diligent hands bring wealth."

PROVERBS 10:4

"Rise and Grind."

CLAY CLARK

DYSFUNCTIONAL MINDSET #2
THE AGGRESSIVE, CRITICAL, AND DEMANDING OF IMMEDIATE IMPOSSIBLE RESULTS ENTREPRENEUR:

You don't like the concept that over a 25 year period of time, one man with diligence could build the state's most successful auto auction, the state's most profitable optometry clinic, one of the state's most successful horse-breeding facilities, a successful durable medical equipment company, a diagnostic sleep center, a booming online business school, and a syndicated radio show... and frankly it irritates you... because you want to build and experience the success of these businesses at once. After all, you see business opportunities everywhere. You've pounded the energy drinks, attended money-magnet seminars, watched the Tony Robbins and Tai Lopez videos and now you want to earn the money that you deserve immediately. You aren't fond of gravity, you believe that you deserve to be able to fly, and you just know that your business idea would go "viral" if you just had the funding.

YOU WANT TO KNOW THE PROVEN PATH UP THE MOUNTAIN TO BUSINESS SUCCESS AND YOU WANT OTHER PEOPLE TO CARRY YOU UP THE MOUNTAIN AS WELL. You want the reward, but you don't want the struggle.

> "Most people are sitting on their own diamond mines. The surest ways to lose your diamond mine are to get bored, become overambitious, or start thinking that the grass is greener on the other side. Find your core focus, stick to it, and devote your time and resources to excelling at it."
>
> **GINO WICKMAN**
> *Best-selling author of Traction: Get a Grip on Your Business*

DYSFUNCTIONAL MINDSET #3
THE CHRONICALLY-DISTRACTED
ENTREPRENEUR:

You want to focus and pay attention, but you just received a notification on your phone that you want to check real quick. You know that you, and you alone, must create the 1,000 words of content that Google needs you to have on every page of your website to enhance your search engine score, but you updated your Facebook status and got into a 45 minute conversation with one of your employees about how they feel instead. You've also recently discovered that it's also very hard to write while watching CNN's non-stop coverage of Hurricane "Who-Gives-A-Crap."

You were trying to read this section of the book, but somebody just liked your Facebook photo and you got distracted...

66

"We need to re-create boundaries. When you carry a digital gadget that creates a virtual link to the office, you need to create a virtual boundary that didn't exist before."

DANIEL GOLEMAN
A world-renowned best-selling author, psychologist, and science journalist. For twelve years, he wrote for The New York Times, reporting on the brain and behavioral sciences. He is the author of the legendary book, Emotional Intelligence.

DYSFUNCTIONAL MINDSET #4
KNOWLEDGEABLE, SKEPTICAL AND COMPLEX BUSINESSES WANT-TO-BE-LEADER:

You graduated from the University of Whatever with a BS (Bachelor of Science) Degree of Whatever, and you have come to the realization that the marketplace does not pay you based upon your academic resume. You know just enough about everything to wow your friends and to engage in an intelligent conversation with any random person that you've ever met on a plane. In the back of your mind, you are thinking... if this doesn't work out, I might need to go back to get my MBA.

You are in love with the vision and goal setting part of business (1% of the work), but you are not in love with the work ethic and process needed to produce the results you seek.

> "You don't get paid for the hour. You get paid for the value you bring to the hour."

JIM ROHN
Best-selling author and famous international speaker / sales trainer

TRUTH CANNON

When I owned the nation's largest wedding entertainment and disc jockey company, I did not know about speakers or how they worked, but I did know how to build a successful business. Doctor Zoellner is not the world's best optometrist and does not actually see patients, yet his business sees more patients than any other optometry clinic in Tulsa. I have no interest in men's grooming, style or haircuts, yet I am a co-founder and CEO of one of the region's most successful chains of men's grooming and haircut lounges, The Elephant In The Room. Doctor Zoellner doesn't know how to maintain cars and does not have an automotive background, yet he owns one of the region's top auto auctions. How is it possible that his auction beats auto auctions owned by lifetime "car guys?" I built the nation's largest wedding photography company, yet I did not know what kind of cameras we used and how to even take photos up until the time I sold it. How is it possible that my photography business is exponentially more successful than the photography company's owned by photography gurus?

DYSFUNCTIONAL MINDSET #5
THE "NEVER ON-TIME" GUY:

Your life is just soooo busy that nobody could possibly understand how busy you are. Although I have five kids, 40 chickens, and 9 businesses, I could never possibly understand how busy you are. Although my own father died of suffocation right in front of my eyes on September 5th, 2016 after a 1 year battle with ALS (Lou Gehrig's disease), I could not possibly understand how stressful your life is. Although my son was born blind, I could never understand how difficult your life is. And because of this, you seek validation and affirmation that somehow the law of sowing and reaping doesn't apply to you because of your "tough situation."

"It doesn't matter if you come from the inner city. People who fail in life are people who find lots of excuses. It's never too late for a person to recognize that they have potential in themselves."

BEN CARSON
A legendary American surgeon whose life was turned into a movie

"Lost time is never found again."

BENJAMIN FRANKLIN
A man who accomplished much during his 84 years on the planet. Benjamin was an American polymath and one of the Founding Fathers of the United States. Franklin was a leading writer, printer, political philosopher, politician, Freemason, postmaster, scientist, inventor, humorist, civic activist, statesman, and diplomat

DYSFUNCTIONAL MINDSET #6
THE "I'M NOT GOING TO DO MY ACTION ITEMS" GUY:

You believe that if you hop on a coaching call and learn the proven system without actually investing your personal time to apply anything eventually things will just get done by themselves. You secretly believe that the science behind the Shake Weight and unicorns is plausible. You believe that your product is so good that it will sell itself and your company will magically build itself without involving you. You have subconsciously bought into the charlatan get-rich-quick-Tai-Lopez-earn-something-for-nothing-so-that-you-can-start-earning-$20,000-per-month-from-home-without-working philosophy of life, which allows you to believe that it is possible to create copious amounts of sustainable wealth without investing the hours of hard work that are required to tediously build workflows, checklists, optimize your website, analyze your web traffic, hire people, fire people, do your accounting, and receive the hundreds of rejections that you need to learn from enroute to actually selling your products at a profit to your ideal and likely buyers.

The 80–100 Hour Work Week

66

"Lazy hands make for poverty, but diligent hands bring wealth."

PROVERBS 10:4

"All hard work brings a profit, but mere talk leads only to poverty."

PROVERBS 14:23

"Yet a little sleep, a little slumber, a little folding of the hands to sleep: So shall thy poverty come as one that travelleth, and thy want as an armed man. A naughty person, a wicked man, walketh with a froward mouth."

PROVERBS 6:10-12

Charlatan

A person who falsely pretends to know or be something in order to deceive people.

> "The three great essentials to achieve anything worthwhile are: Hard work, stick-to-itiveness, and common sense."

> "Genius is one percent inspiration and ninety-nine percent perspiration."

THOMAS EDISON

Many consider him to be the world's best inventor and half of you reading this consider him to be the man who stole Tesla's light bulb invention. He developed many devices that greatly influenced life around the world, including the phonograph, the motion picture camera, and the long-lasting, practical electric light bulb. Dubbed "The Wizard of Menlo Park."

Edison was one of the first inventors to apply the principles of mass production and large-scale teamwork to the process of invention, and because of that, he is often credited with the creation of the first industrial research laboratory. Edison held 1,093 US patents in his name, as well as patents all over the world. He founded General Electric and is responsible for essentially creating the industries involving: electric light, power utilities, recorded sound and the motion pictures (movies). It's arguable that without Edison, we would not have electric light, recorded sound, recorded motion pictures, or movies.

DYSFUNCTIONAL MINDSET #7
THE "NON-EMOTIONALLY ENGAGED" GUY:

You don't want to admit that you are stuck and that you need help breaking through your biggest limiting factors, but you do recognize that you "may need some coaching" so you hesitantly have enrolled in a business coaching platform so that you can "try it out." You won't engage in the conversations with your coach or ever knock out your action items... because you are just seeing if this program can help you... This logic makes sense to you... I'm going to try out farming. I'm not going to do the hard work required to till the soil, to sow the seeds, or to water the seeds. I just want to see what this farming thing is all about and if the "tilling, sowing, watering, and reaping" theory actually works.

You want the financial freedom, the corner office, and time freedom that you will get as a result of producing a boatload of profits, but you are not willing to suffer through the sixty-hour workweeks filled with endless sales calls, staff recruitment, detailed paperwork, training, and workflow creation.

66
....

"Lazy hands make for poverty, but diligent hands bring wealth."

PROVERBS 10:4
From that controversial book known as The Bible

DYSFUNCTIONAL MINDSET #8
THE "I'M-GOING-TO-TRY-TO-SOLVE-ALL-OF-MY-BUSINESS-QUESTIONS-AT-ONCE" GUY:

You want to SOLVE ALL OF YOUR BUSINESS PROBLEMS NOW although every successful entrepreneur on the planet will tell you that you must simplify and focus on methodically knocking out the action items that will (move-the-needle) create the biggest impact in your business. For you, my friend, you must understand that the process of building a successful business is just that...a process.

> "People think focus means saying yes to the thing you've got to focus on. But that's not what it means at all. It means saying no to the hundred other good ideas that there are. You have to pick carefully. I'm actually as proud of the things we haven't done as the things I have done. Innovation is saying no to 1,000 things."

STEVE JOBS
Co-founder of Apple and the former CEO of PIXAR

DYSFUNCTIONAL MINDSET #9
THE "EVERYTHING IS A BURNING FIRE" GUY:

You have never consistently blocked out the 1 to 2 hours per day that are REQUIRED to intentionally design a successful life one day and one action item at a time. You have not yet created the habit of diligently mapping out your day in a place and at a time where you will be un-interrupted by distractions. Thus, you are currently trying to do the impossible. You aren't blocking out the "quiet time," "planning time" or "meta-time" (the 2 hours of daily planning time) that every top entrepreneur needs for proactively planning out their day. Thus, the success that Lee Cockerell, Doctor Zoellner, and I have achieved is currently not possible for you. So...you secretly always feel like you are "running behind" and that everything is a burning fire. As your business grows, this will become an increasingly massive problem and will likely cause you to have a mental break-down at some point. I've seen this happen countless times. My friend, you must start proactively planning out and designing each successful day for your successful life. This "my-hair-is-on-fire" approach to life is going to keep you busy and furiously thrashing about without moving forward.

66

"One way to get your priorities accomplished is to schedule them into your calendar."

LEE COCKERELL
The former Executive President of Walt Disney World Resorts that used to manage 40,000 cast members as the former Executive Vice President of Operations for Walt Disney World Resorts

DYSFUNCTIONAL MINDSET #10
THE "CONSTANTLY-CALLING-TEXTING-AND-EMAILING- WITH-URGENT-ACTION-ITEMS" GUY:

You are new to business success and because 8 out of 10 businesses fail (according to Forbes), you've never personally witnessed the nitty-gritty details of somebody actually starting and growing a successful business firsthand, so this whole scheduled "meeting-once-a-week-thing" really frustrates you. You want to believe that Doctor Zoellner and I have created financial and time freedom by being accessible to each other and every member of our team 24-7. You want to believe that the REAL SECRET to our success has been just running from one burning fire to the next...and fortunately, that is not true. In fact, Doctor Zoellner and I don't email each other EVER unless it's to share a legal document. In fact, Doctor Zoellner and I don't text each other all day with show notes for our radio show, pictures of cats, or random burning fires. We have scheduled weekly times to meet with who we need to meet with. We have scheduled "rocks" into our schedule that must happen and we know the "Key Performance Indicators" that we must hold our teammates accountable to EVERYDAY.

> "Successful businesses operate with a crystal clear vision that is shared by everyone. They have the right people in the right seats. They have a pulse on their operations by watching and managing a handful of numbers on a weekly basis. They identify and solve issues promptly in an open and honest environment. They document their processes and ensure that they are followed by everyone. They establish priorities for each employee and ensure that a high level of trust, communication, and accountability exists on each team."

GINO WICKMAN
Best-selling author of Traction

DYSFUNCTIONAL MINDSET #11
THE "MAD-AT-THE-MESSENGER" GUY:

The former communist leaders of the Soviet Union thought that the systematic redistribution of wealth through a government-mandated system was a great idea. They really didn't like it when they surveyed their people and found that most of their population was either unmotivated, literally starving, or passionately longing to go back to a time where the government didn't control everything. Thus, when their citizens told them negative feedback, they killed them. The people of planet Earth didn't like it when Jesus came to Earth and pointed out the truth, so they killed him. Racist people didn't like that Martin Luther King Jr. dared to say, "I have a dream that my four little children will one day live in a nation where they will not be judged by the color of their skin, but by the content of their character," so they assassinated him. So you now are tempted to do this same move, "attack-the-messenger."

With this mindset, when you hear uncomfortable truths about your business, you realize that this is the perfect time to attack the character or the resume of the coach presenting you with the simplicity and diligence required to implement the proven 13-point business system that both Doctor Zoellner and I have designed for ourselves and that we are now, for the first time, teaching to others like you.

> "If you are going to tell people the truth, you had better be funny or it won't go over well."
>
> **LEE COCKERELL**
> *The former Executive Vice President of Walt Disney World Resorts who once successfully managed 40,000 employees and all of the personality types that comes with a large workforce*

SUPER MOVES: HOW TO BE FUNNY

1. Shock and Awe / Physical Comedy
2. Self-Depreciation
3. Recovery
4. Jokes
5. Stories

The Time Will Never be Just Right

"

"For all of the most important things, the timing always sucks. Waiting for a good time to quit your job? The stars will never align and the traffic lights of life will never all be green at the same time. The universe doesn't conspire against you, but it doesn't go out of its way to line up the pins either. Conditions are never perfect. "Someday" is a disease that will take your dreams to the grave with you. Pro and con lists are just as bad. If it's important to you and you want to do it "eventually," just do it and correct course along the way."

TIM FERRISS
Best-selling author of the Four Hour Work Week, former venture capitalist, and one of the world's most successful podcasters

Put a check mark by the excuse that seems like the most viable reason that you cannot possibly become successful.

☐ Too Young

☐ Too Old

☐ No Connections

☐ No Capital

☐ No Time

☐ No Skills

☐ No ability to Focus

☐ Have to Wait Until Kids Go to School

☐ Don't Do Well with People

☐ Love People Too Much

☐ Afraid of Success

☐ Afraid of Failure

☐ Attention Deficit Disorder

☐ Obsessive Compulsive Disorder

☐ Too Chronically Fatigued

DYSFUNCTIONAL MINDSET #12
THE "I-CARE-ABOUT-WHAT-EVERYBODY-ELSE-THINKS-AND-SO-TO-AVOID-ANY-CONFRONTATION-EVER-I-NEVER-HOLD-PEOPLE-ACCOUNTABLE-NEVER-TAKE-A-STAND-FOR-ANYTHING-NEVER-FIRE-ANYBODY-AND-NEVER-CREATE-REMARKABLE-MARKETING-AND-COMPELLING-NO-BRAINER-OFFERS-NEEDED-TO-GET-YOUR-IDEAL-AND-LIKELY-BUYERS-TO-TAKE-THE-ACTION-YOU-WANT" GUY:

You've always been "a pleaser," and, generally, a well-liked person. Because you are not a psychopath, you actually have always cared about people, how you make people feel, and how people feel about you.

However, as an aspiring entrepreneur you have begun to realize that this "please everybody first" and "make sure everybody likes my idea before I do anything" mentality has consistently caused you to do nothing in an attempt to avoid criticism. If this is you, these are the repetitive problems that you find yourself dealing with every day:

Psychopath
A person who is mentally ill, who does not care about other people, and who is usually dangerous or violent.

1. You struggle deciding on the market niche that you will focus on and cater to because you worry about excluding people that may get offended.

2. You struggle to launch aggressive marketing.

> "Being responsible sometimes means pissing people off."
> **COLIN POWELL**

> "In a crowded marketplace, fitting in is failing. In a busy marketplace, not standing out is the same as being invisible...If you're remarkable, then it's likely that some people won't like you. That's part of the definition of remarkable. Nobody gets unanimous praise -- ever. The best the timid can hope for is to be unnoticed. Criticism comes to those who stand out. Playing it safe. Following the rules. They seem like the best ways to avoid failure. Alas, that pattern is awfully dangerous. The current marketing "rules" will ultimately lead to failure."

SETH GODIN
Best-selling author and marketing guru who sold his business Yoyodyne to Yahoo! For $30 million

Ample Examples of Purple Cows:

The pricing of Starbucks coffee.

- Iced Coffee (with or without Milk) – Tall – $2.25
- Iced Coffee (with or without Milk) – Grande – $2.65
- Iced Coffee (with or without Milk) – Venti – $2.95
- Iced Coffee (with or without Milk) – Trenta – $3.45

The pricing of Apple products.

The jokes, pricing and advertising strategies of Southwest Airlines (do a Google search for "Southwest airlines flight attendant rap" and you will see what I'm talking about).

The volume, loudness and all-around testosterone of the Harley Davidson motorcycles.

The refusal of In-n-Out Burger to add chicken and ANY other items to their menu and their refusal to stop printing the Bible verses on their packaging (Proverbs 3:5, John 3:16, Revelation 3:20 and Nahum 1:7).

- "Trust in the LORD with all your heart and lean not on your own understanding." – Proverbs 3:5

- "For God so loved the world that he gave his one and only Son, that whoever believes in him shall not perish but have eternal life." – John 3:16

- "Here I am! I stand at the door and knock. If anyone hears my voice and opens the door, I will come in and eat with that person, and they with me." – Revelation 3:20

- "The Lord is good, a refuge in times of trouble. He cares for those who trust in him." – Nahum 1:7

The pricing of Champagne Armand de Brignac – $299 per bottle.

The Marriott Hotel's insistence on putting The Bible and the Book of Mormon in every hotel room.

1. Because you worry that it may upset your competition or somebody else inhabiting the planet Earth. In your mind, you often say, "I don't know if I should say that in my CALL TO ACTION OR HEADLINE because technically our service or product actually includes A, B, C and D, not just A, B and C…"

"Don't be distracted by criticism. Remember, the only taste of success some people have is when they take a bite out of you."

ZIG ZIGLAR
Best-selling author, motivational speaker, and legendary sales trainer

2. You struggle choosing the overhead music that is played in your office because Kevin keeps saying, "It's like we've heard the same songs every day. CAN WE PLEASE CHANGE THE MUSIC!"

> "Great spirits have always encountered violent opposition from mediocre minds."
>
> **ALBERT EINSTEIN**
> *A German-born theoretical physicist. He developed the general theory of relativity, one of the two pillars of modern physics (alongside quantum mechanics)*

3. You struggle to get your staff to follow any expectations that you have for them. Your team members run around doing whatever they want regardless of what is outlined in your handbook. They don't follow your dress code, any processes, or any systems that you have ever created and thus, you always find yourself doing everything yourself because "they may not like being told what to do."

> "Be candid with everyone."
>
> **JACK WELCH**
> *The legendary CEO of GE who grew the company by 4,000% during his tenure*

1. You struggle to hold your staff accountable to being on time because you worry about them saying, "TRAFFIC WAS TERRIBLE," "LOOK I GOT TO WORK AS SOON AS I COULD," "I FORGOT" or "I'M SO SORRY I OVERSLEPT." You actually have created a business where you feel as though your staff owns the business because they tell you what hours they will work and what jobs they are willing to do.

> "Jesus entered the temple courts and drove out all who were buying and selling there. He overturned the tables of the money changers and the benches of those selling doves. "It is written," he said to them, "'My house will be called a house of prayer,' but you are making it 'a den of robbers."
>
> **MATTHEW 21:12-13**

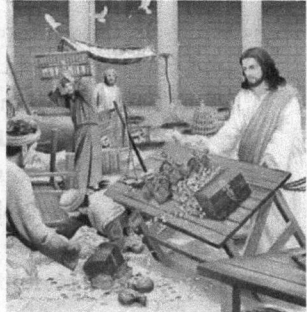

2. You struggle to raise prices to a profitable level, so you just slave away working hard without making a profit because you worry about what your customers will say.

> "Sales are contingent upon the attitude of the salesman, not the attitude of the prospect."
>
> **WILLIAM CLEMENT STONE**
> *Best selling author and sales expert*

LIVE WITHOUT BOUNDARIES

"Caring about what everybody thinks is bad for your mental health. Doing this will cause you live a life without boundaries and to dedicate your living hours to chasing the impossible goal of pleasing everybody, responding to every email, every text message, and offending no one. The key to being happy is getting yourself to a point where you are intentional about what and who you care about and being intentional about what you don't care about. Only after you have invested the time to determine your values and your goals related to your faith, family, friendships, fitness, fun, and finances will you be able to truly know what and who you should care about. My friend, you must care about something. But you must only care about what truly matters. Your faith. Your family. Your friendships. Your fitness. Your fun. Your finances. Your New England Patriots. It's absolutely impossible to become a successful person without becoming the butt of the jokes made by your critics. To truly get to the place where you sincerely do not care about what most people think, you must firmly know your goals and where you are going with your life."

CLAY TIBERIUS CLARK
The former U.S. SBA Entrepreneur of the Year, the father of the 5 human kids, the raiser of 40 chickens, and America's most pale male

"Every sale has five basic obstacles: no need, no money, no hurry, no desire, no trust."

ZIG ZIGLAR
Best selling author and sales expert

"There is only one way to avoid criticism: do nothing, say nothing, and be nothing."

ARISTOTLE
(The famous Greek philosopher)

1. You struggle to get your staff to pay attention in meetings, to stop texting while at work, to stay off of their cell phones, and to stop updating their social media accounts during the work day because you worry about what "they" may say when you call "them" out.

You will Create Enemies if You are Honest

66 ....

"You have enemies? Good. That means you've stood up for something sometime in your life."

WINSTON CHURCHILL
The Prime Minister of the United Kingdom from 1940 to 1945 who led the British in their fight against Adolf Hitler and Nazi Germany. He also led the country from 1951 to 1955. Churchill was an officer in the British Army, a non-academic historian, a writer (as Winston S. Churchill), and an artist. He won the Nobel Prize in Literature in 1953 for his overall, lifetime body of work.

66 ....

"10 Blessed are they which are persecuted for righteousness' sake: for theirs is the kingdom of heaven. 11 Blessed are ye, when men shall revile you, and persecute you, and shall say all manner of evil against you falsely, for my sake."

- MATTHEW 5:10-11
The Book of Matthew was written by the Apostle Matthew who was a tax collector before becoming one of Jesus' trusted twelve disciples. Throughout the book Matthew, Matthew demonstrates that he has a vast knowledge of geography, Jewish customs, and the Old Testament prophecies. The book of Matthew discusses the birth of Jesus, the miracles of Jesus, the crucifixion of Jesus and the resurrection of Jesus.

WHY IS THE MATTRESS BUSINESS SUCH A SLEEPER?

"Opportunity is missed by most people because it is dressed in overalls and looks like work."

THOMAS EDISON
The inverter of recorded video, recorded audio, the modern lightbulb, and the founder of General Electric.

"If you're wrong, you will die. But most companies don't die because they are wrong; most die because they don't commit themselves. They fritter away their valuable resources while attempting to make a decision. The greatest danger is in standing still."

-Andy Grove
(Founding team member and the former CEO of Intel)

DEEP THOUGHTS
FROM THE
MATTRESS KING

""

This book is the cumulation of all my knowledge and experience about selling mattresses at a sustainable profit.

— *Darren Conrad*

"No one lives long enough to learn everything they need to learn starting from scratch. To be successful, we absolutely, positively have to find people who have already paid the price to learn the things that we need to learn to achieve our goals."

BRIAN TRACY

(The legendary bestselling author, sales trainer, and speaker.)

DEEP THOUGHTS FROM THE MATTRESS KING

66 99

When you're running your own business, things will happen, both good and bad. Your choice is to either look at the problem or the solution. If you look for the problem, the problem will get bigger. If you look for the solution, the solution will get bigger.

—— *Darren Conrad* ——

THE BACKSTORY (SWEET DREAMS)

Can You Achieve Your Financial Goals By Selling Mattresses?!

YES! You Can! This book is designed to give you a behind the scenes look into our business model and to show you our origin story of how we began. Let's get started!

The mattress business is the last thing that I ever planned on getting into. After graduating high school, I began to sell Cutco knives with a company called "Vector Marketing" in Columbus, Ohio. When I first got started selling Cutco, I had to come up with a list of all the people that I knew that I could go practice with, which included friends and family. I had to call them up, schedule a time to go to their house and meet them, do my presentation and then ask them for referrals. When I first got started, I tried so hard to be a successful sales person. I read the book, *Secrets of Closing the Sale*, by Zig Ziglar and I wanted to just be great at selling Cutco. I was trying too hard to SELL and it backfired because nobody would buy from me. Being in this position, I asked my manager for help. He told me to just be authentic and genuine and help people out. He suggested the book, *How to Win Friends and Influence People*, by Dale Carnegie. When I was just naturally having fun with people helping them out, my sales skyrocketed. I quickly learned that people don't want to be sold, they want to make a decision to buy from you. It was at this point that I learned being authentic and genuinely helping others is a great formula for success.

I had no idea the impact that selling Cutco would have on my life. It taught me perseverance. It taught me how to handle rejection, set goals and the importance of believing in what you're doing or what product you represent. If you believe in something and it's good and it helps others, then success is inevitable. Driving around the city, going to peoples homes and doing in-home presentations, asking for leads, knocking on doors and creating a consistent weekly plan. I learned that selling Cutco is like running a marathon. It's not a sprint, and if you follow the system consistently, you'll continue to get results year round. With the success of selling Cutco, I was promoted to district manager. I then moved north to Cleveland, Ohio. I rented an office space with a training room. I hired secretaries and I started the process of teaching people to sell Cutco the way that I did as a sales rep. I was interviewing, recruiting, and training college kids to sell Cutco knives. During this time, I was also developing myself professionally in the cutlery business. I learned how to speak publicly, how to set goals, and how to work in an efficient manner. It was a great experience and I had a lot of success. Ultimately, I became one of the top branch offices in the company while running this business.

During that time, I was often asked where I went to college, and I would tell them that I had not gone to college. A friend of mine suggested that I apply to Ohio State. I was twenty-four at the time and I decided to go for it. I closed down my Vector office and I decided to get a four-year degree in business marketing. After college, I used my previous work experience with Cutco knives as well as my college degree to get into the pharmaceutical and medical supply business.

"A Carnegie or a Rockefeller or a James J. Hill or a Marshall Field accumulates a fortune through the application of the same principles available to all of us, but we envy them and their wealth without ever thinking of studying their philosophy and applying it to ourselves. We look at a successful person in the hour of their triumph and wonder how they did it, but we overlook the importance of analyzing their methods, and we forget the price they had to pay in the careful and well-organized preparation that had to be made before they could reap the fruits of their efforts."

NAPOLEON HILL

(The Best-selling author of Think & Grow Rich and the number one best-selling self-help author of all time.)

The former CEO of Vector Marketing reached out to me and asked me to work with his new website company as a regional coordinator. The company was called www.CollegeClub.com and was very similar to what Facebook is today. My role was to visit college campuses across the United States and promote this community. After a year and a half of working with the company, I bought my first house and I felt like I was on my way to success.

Unfortunately, that's when the company went out of business. So, here I am after purchasing my first house, and suddenly, I don't have a job anymore. At that point, a friend of mine reached out to me. He was selling mattresses out of a storage unit and he suggested that I join him. This was the very last thing I wanted to do, but with no other option at the time, I decided to go for it and get into the mattress business. I didn't want to use a storage unit, so instead, I rented an 800-square-foot storefront off the beaten path for $800 a month. I started posting ads, and my business took off!

I began to tell my friends who formerly worked for www.CollegeClub.com and Vector Marketing, and they all joined me in the mattress business as well. This was the beginning of my journey into the mattress business.

"Start where you are, with what you have. Make something of it and never be satisfied."

GEORGE WASHINGTON CARVER

(A man who was born into slavery and who became the legendary self-taught American botanist and inventor who actively promoted the alternative crops and methods that lead to the prevention of soil mineral depletion for African Americans. Before George Washington Carver, newly freed African Americans did not know how to raise crops that would not deplete their lands of vital nutrients and essential minerals.)

After working in the mattress business for a while, I started to realize what a fantastic business it was. I started to realize that it was much bigger than what I expected at the beginning. It was profitable, it was fun, and I still believe it is the greatest business in America. I got to make my own schedule and be in control of my time, which, to me, was freedom. I got to help people get a great product at a great value. I also made a significant income, which was nice too. It reminds me of a story:

A Texas billionaire wanted to have a coming out party for his daughter. He invited all the eligible bachelors in the area to come to his mansion estate. He brought them all outside to an Olympic size swimming pool area filled with alligators and water moccasins, and he offered them a challenge. He said to men, "If anyone can jump in the pool and swim to the other side, I will give them a choice of one of the following things. One- he could have my beautiful daughter's hand in marriage. Two- he could have $1 million dollars. Or three- he could have the deed to my estate." As soon as the billionaire said the last offer, he heard a big splash at the end of the pool. There was Johnny- fighting, swimming, maneuvering, and getting to the distance of the pool. When Johnny got out of the pool, the Texas billionaire was surprised that someone actually jumped in and swam the entire distance of the pool. The billionaire said, "Young man, I'm a man of my word, and I will give you one of three things. Would you like my beautiful daughter's hand in marriage?" Johnny said, "No sir." The billionaire said, "Son, would you like $1 million?" And Johnny said, "No sir" with a smile and grin. The Texas billionaire said, "Well son, would you like the deed to my estate?" And Johnny said, "No sir." The billionaire said, "Son, what do you want?" Johnny said, "I'd like to know the fella that pushed me in the pool!" The point of the story is however you found the mattress business, you got brought into this business. Take advantage of the opportunity in front of you!

After working with my friend in Columbus, Ohio, building his business from 2000 to 2003, I decided to start my own business. I sold my house and rental properties, took all of my cash and belongings and I picked up and moved to Greenville, South Carolina, and started my first mattress company on my own.

Through overcoming trials and challenges the past twenty-five years, I have built six different companies teaching and training people how to run their own business and how to follow the business model I learned while at Vector Marketing, using my skills and knowledge that I have gained in the Cutco knife business. America Bedding Direct is going to be the greatest of all.

I'm excited to take you on this incredible journey that will change your life. At the beginning, I had no idea how much I would love this business. Twenty-five years later, I continue to teach and train people the same business model that changed my life. For the complete story you can read my book, *The Rugged Roadtrip.*

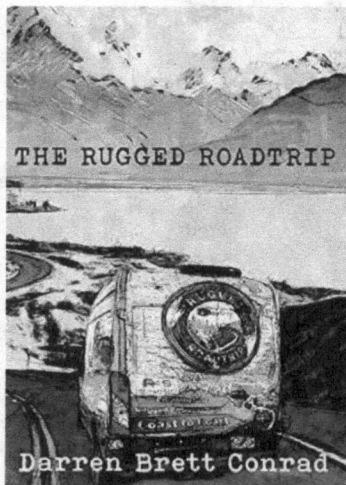

CHAPTER 1

GETTING STARTED

(WAKE UP CALL)

"Vision without execution is hallucination."

THOMAS EDISON

(The man who introduced the world to recorded audio, recorded video, the first practical lightbulb, GE, and countless other inventions and business concepts.)

In this book, you will learn exactly what you need to do every single step of the way in order to be successful. Our formula is simple and has been used for over three decades. We have mastered this simple business, so all you need to do is follow the guidance we offer, be teachable and plug into the Clay Clark business coaching system. We provide all the resources, mentorship and accountability you need to be successful, and we have provided easy-to-follow instructions to guide you through each aspect of the business.

"Work like most people will not, so you can live like most people cannot."

DAVE RAMSEY

(The legendary best-selling author, entrepreneur, radio talk show host, podcaster, financial guru, speaker and financial trainer.)

Attitude is Everything.

There's a fantastic quote from Charles Swindoll:

"The longer I live, the more I realize the impact of attitude on life. Attitude, to me, is more important than facts. It's more important than past, than education, than money, than circumstances, than failures, than successes, than what other people think, say or do. It is more important than appearance, giftedness, or skill. It will make or break a company... a church... a home. The remarkable thing is we have a choice everyday regarding the attitude we embrace for that day. We cannot change our past. We cannot change the fact that people will act in a certain way. We cannot change the inevitable. The only thing we can do is play on the one string we have and that's our attitude. I'm convinced that life is 10% of what happens to me and 90% of how I react to it. And so it is with you. We are in charge of our attitudes."

CHUCK SWINDOLL

(Charles Rozell Swindoll is a well known evangelical Christian pastor, author, educator, and radio preacher. He founded an organization called Insight for Living, which is headquartered in Frisco, Texas, which airs a radio program of the same name on more than 2,000 radio stations around the world, which is then broadcast in 15 different languages.)

When you're running your own business, things will happen both good and bad. Your choice is to either look at the problem or the solution. You should have an attitude of "what can I do to solve this problem?" If you look for the problem, the problem will get bigger. If you look for the solution, the solution will get bigger. My advice would be to always be focused on the solution.

A good example of this could be the following: you're expecting a truck to deliver your inventory on a Monday, but an unavoidable delay happens causing the truck to arrive late on Thursday. Nothing that you do is going to change the fact that your truck is going to be arriving late. So how do you respond to it? Well, you could pack up, close your store, and choose not to work, or you could continue to fight through these issues as best as you possibly can. The best solution in this case would be to meet your customers, let them know the situation, and give them a discount when they pick up the mattress on Thursday. You could also let them know how it's difficult to keep inventory on hand with prices so low and everything going so fast. Most of the time, people understand this.

"The size of your success is measured by the strength of your desire; the size of your dream; and how you handle disappointment along the way."

ROBERT KIYOSAKI

(Robert Kiyosaki is an international best-selling author of the Rich Dad Poor Dad book series, a legendary real estate investor, multiple-time ThrivetimeShow.com podcast guest, and entrepreneur. Kiyosaki is the author of more than 26 books, including the international self-published personal finance Rich Dad Poor Dad series of books which has been translated into 51 languages and sold over 41 million copies worldwide.)

> ## "You are the average of the five people you spend the most time with."

JIM ROHN

(The legendary self-help guru, best-selling author and mentor to Tony Robbins. Jim Rohn mentored Mark R. Hughes (the founder of Herbalife International) and life strategist Tony Robbins in the late 1970s. Others who credit Rohn for influencing their careers include authors/lecturers Mark Victor Hansen, Jack Canfield (Chicken Soup book series), Everton Edwards (Hallmark Innovators Conglomerate), Brian Tracy, Darren Hardy, Todd Smith, Kevin Garver, and T. Harv Eker. Rohn coauthored the novel Twelve Pillars with Chris Widener.)

I want to do an exercise with you that I learned from Tony Robbins. Pretend like you're depressed; go sit and act like you're depressed. How would your body change? You'd be slumped over, frowning, your head would be down, etc. Now let's do something different- I want you to put a big smile on your face while at the same time trying to act depressed. It is impossible. You cannot smile and be depressed at the same time. Your mind will follow your physiology. Practice smiling on a daily basis and even practice doing smiling exercises—it actually works! Sometimes in business, you have to get tough, put a smile on your face, and look for a solution. With the right attitude, you'll be more successful than with the wrong attitude. Life is going to happen; don't react to it. It's all about responding to the challenges in a positive way.

Another thing that I learned from Tony Robbins is this: Focus on what questions you are asking yourself. Whatever questions you're asking yourself, your mind will answer. If you're asking yourself, "Why am I always broke?," you're always going to answer that question. If you start asking positive questions like, "What can I do to be more financially successful?," that is a much more empowering question. Pay attention to the questions that you ask yourself, and make sure that you're asking yourself empowering questions rather than negative questions. You should be asking yourself questions like, "What can I do to dominate my business market and be more successful? What can I do to create more customers? What can I do to have fun while building a business?" I've included a list of some books that I've read that really impacted my life:

» *How to Win Friends and Influence People*, by Dale Carnegie

» *How to Become Sustainably Rich*, by Clay Clark

» *Excuse Me Your Life Is Waiting*, by Lynn Grabhorn

» *Awaken The Giant Within*, by Tony Robbins

» *The Surrender Experiment*, by Michael Singer

» *Think and Grow Rich*, by Napoleon Hill

"The key is not to prioritize what's on your schedule, but to schedule your priorities."

STEPHEN COVEY

(An American educator, author, businessman, and keynote speaker. His most popular book was the New York Times best-selling book, The 7 Habits of Highly Effective People.)

"Persistence trumps talent. What's the most powerful force in the universe? Compound interest. It builds on itself. Over time, a small amount of money becomes a large amount of money. Persistence is similar. A little bit improves performance, which encourages greater persistence, which improves persistence even more. And on and on it goes. Lack of persistence works the same way -- only in the opposite direction."

DANIEL PINK

(A www.ThrivetimeShow.com Podcast guest, a seven times New York Times bestseller, and the host and a co-executive producer of the National Geographic Channel social science TV series Crowd Control.)

Remember, our business is not like a typical mattress store. We teach everything the exact opposite of the way that a retail store would do. That means that when you tell your friends and family that you're getting into the mattress business, I would suggest not listening to their suggestions or their ideas on how to be successful. In general, you should avoid SNIOPS (Susceptible to Negative Influence of Other People.) I also encourage people to avoid watching the news, which typically pumps you full of facts about how bad the economy is or how bad business is, etc. You must remember to focus on things that will empower you and lead you to be successful.

"Most people spend more time planning a vacation than they do planning a life."

CHET HOLMES

(The legendary business consultant and the best-selling author of The Ultimate Sales Machine. Chet Holmes was a business associate of Warren Buffet's business partner, Charlie Munger.)

Income Potential

Learning how to sell mattresses is public information and easily available online. There are many ways to buy and sell mattresses. There are no secrets or magical formulas. The great differentiator is hard work and execution. Taking action; this is the "secret" to earning a six-figure yearly income by selling mattresses. It's easy, but it does require work. It is very simple: advertise, respond to the customer, meet the customer, repeat. Make sure to track your business in the process.

"When you want to succeed as bad as you want to breathe, then you'll be successful."

ERIC THOMAS

(A www.ThrivetimeShow.com Podcast guest, motivational speaker, author, and consultant.)

Know Your Numbers to Grow Your Numbers!

You must track your business daily—small changes can make a huge impact on your yearly income

	EXPENSES	INCOME
WEEKLY SALES ($150)		
15	$1,500	$39,000
25	$1,500	$117,000
35	$1,500	$195,000
45	$1,500	$273,000
WEEKLY SALES ($200)		
15	$2,000	$52,000
25	$2,000	$156,000
35	$2,000	$260,000
45	$2,000	$364,000
WEEKLY SALES ($250)		
15	$2,500	$65,000
25	$2,500	$195,000
35	$2,500	$325,000
45	$2,500	$455,000

Business Philosophy

There is a big difference between retail stores and our business:

Location- Regular retail mattress stores usually take up 5,000 square feet and cost $8,000-$10,000/month in rent or more. In contrast, our locations are very simple. It is usually around 1,000-2,000 sq. ft. The average location's monthly rent is $1,200-$3,000, meaning we have low overhead. We make sure to find a location that is easy to give directions to, safe to go to at night, and low in rent.

Product- Typical mattress retailers carry forty to fifty floor model mattress choices and four or more major different brands. This makes buying a mattress from a store very difficult and overwhelming. That is why less than 20% of the people who walk into a mattress store actually make a purchase. On the other hand, we have only 7 to 10 styles to choose from in our locations. We offer high-quality firm, medium and soft mattresses in all sizes. These mattresses are lined up in order from highest price to lowest price, highest price being by the door. Having more than 10 choices and multiple mattress vendors is much harder to manage and operate. We keep it simple and efficient.

Price- Our prices at our shop are significantly lower than traditional mattress stores. For a queen-size mattress set that a customer would pay $400 in a store, we sell for $250. For a queen-size set that would retail for $1,200, we sell for $450. For mattresses with special features such as pocketed coils and visco memory foam that would sell in stores for $2,600, we sell for $900. We give our customers a huge discount.

Marketing/Sales Process- Our marketing and sales process is totally opposite of the retail mattress locations. We advertise with a sense of urgency. Additionally, we advertise a contact instead of an address. The customer calls us and needs a mattress. We give them the location and they meet us there to pick out the mattress they want. The sales process only takes five to ten minutes, and we never do any high pressure selling. We turn our product inventory on a weekly basis.

"Implementation, not ideas, is the key to real success."

CHET HOLMES

(The legendary business consultant and the best-selling author of The Ultimate Sales Machine.)

DEEP THOUGHTS FROM THE MATTRESS KING

— **"**　**"** —

Remember, we are not a typical mattress store. We sell closeouts, clearance, and overstock items, and we are available by appointment only.

——— Darren Conrad ———

The Biblical Ten Commandments
(Found In Exodus Chapter 20: 3-17):

Commandment #1 - [3] Thou shalt have no other gods before me. [4] Thou shalt not make unto thee any graven image, or any likeness of any thing that is in heaven above, or that is in the earth beneath, or that is in the water under the earth. [5] Thou shalt not bow down thyself to them, nor serve them: for I the Lord thy God am a jealous God, visiting the iniquity of the fathers upon the children unto the third and fourth generation of them that hate me; [6] And shewing mercy unto thousands of them that love me, and keep my commandments.

Commandment #2 - [7] Thou shalt not take the name of the Lord thy God in vain; for the Lord will not hold him guiltless that taketh his name in vain.

Commandment #3 - [8] Remember the sabbath day, to keep it holy.

Commandment #4 - [9] Six days shalt thou labour, and do all thy work: [10] But the seventh day is the sabbath of the Lord thy God: in it thou shalt not do any work, thou, nor thy son, nor thy daughter, thy manservant, nor thy maidservant, nor thy cattle, nor thy stranger that is within thy gates: [11] For in six days the Lord made heaven and earth, the sea, and all that in them is, and rested the seventh day: wherefore the Lord blessed the sabbath day, and hallowed it.

Commandment #5 - [12] Honour thy father and thy mother: that thy days may be long upon the land which the Lord thy God giveth thee.

Commandment #6 - [13] Thou shalt not kill.

Commandment #7 - [14] Thou shalt not commit adultery.

Commandment #8 - [15] Thou shalt not steal.

Commandment #9 - [16] Thou shalt not bear false witness against thy neighbour.

Commandment #10 - [17] Thou shalt not covet thy neighbour's house, thou shalt not covet thy neighbour's wife, nor his manservant, nor his maidservant, nor his ox, nor his ass, nor any thing that is thy neighbour's.

The American Bedding Direct 10 Commandments for Achieving Success:

Commandment #1 - Thou shall take responsibility for the success or failure of your business.

Commandment #2 - Thou shall urgently secure a commercial location for your business.

Commandment #3 - Thou shall urgently register a Google Map within your local designated market area.

Commandment #4 - Thou shall gather two times more objective Google reviews than any of the local mattress business competitors within your designated market area.

Commandment #5 - Thou shall diligently meet with your business coach each week to learn what action items you need to take to earn the money you want to make.

Commandment #6 - Thou shall block out the time needed to turn your to-do list into a to-done list.

Commandment #7 - Thou shall gather two times more objective Google reviews than any of the local mattress business competitors within your designated market area.

Commandment #8 - Thou shall measure what you treasure and track where you don't want your business to slack.

Commandment #9 - Thou shall call, text and email your leads until they cry, buy or die.

Commandment #10 - Thou shall gather two times more objective Google reviews than any of the local mattress business competitors within your designated market area.

DEEP THOUGHTS FROM THE MATTRESS KING

—————— 66 99 ——————

"Dream Big, Trust GOD and Always Smile!"

"Trust in the Lord with all your heart and lean not on your own understanding; in all your ways submit to him, and he will make your paths straight."

— Proverbs 3:5-6

——————— *Darren Conrad* ———————

CHAPTER 2

SETTING UP

(YOU WON'T TOSS AND TURN AFTER YOU LEARN HOW TO SET UP PROPERLY)

Finding Space— We look for an empty rectangle 1,000-2,000 square-foot space. Typically, we want to look for a location somewhere close to home. We are looking for a place that is easy to find and in a safe neighborhood. A fifty-three foot truck must have access for weekly deliveries. Remember, we are a destination location, not a retail store, so it doesn't really matter if it is a high traffic street or not. The first step in looking for space is just driving around and searching for business parks, strip malls, industrial parks and empty retail space off of the Main Street.

Choose locations that are safe to go to after dark.

Contact the listing realtor and let them know what you are looking for, they can suggest other properties. Search the internet for retail/warehouse space for rent; Loopnet.com is a great resource for finding space too, however, it does not include private owners that are renting space.

Do not rely solely on them to find space for you, continue to search on your own.

$10-$15 per square foot is ideal.

Once you find potential space, we can help you negotiate the lease.

"Knowledge is the key that unlocks all the doors. You can be green-skinned with yellow polka dots and come from Mars, but if you have knowledge that people need, instead of beating you, they'll beat a path to your door."

BEN CARSON

(A ThrivetimeShow.com Podcast guest, an American retired neurosurgeon, academic, author, and government official who served as the 17th United States secretary of housing and urban development from 2017 to 2021. A pioneer in the field of neurosurgery, he was a candidate for President of the United States in the 2016 Republican primaries. Carson is one of the most prominent black conservatives in the United States.)

Showroom Setup Guide

» NO channel letter signage on the building.

  › Instead, use a vinyl cling on the front door that includes business name, phone number, address, and "Schedule to View Inventory."

» Display mattresses in order by price from high to low starting from the front door.

» Remove mattress from plastic by opening at the top and pulling down like a sock. That way, the mattress can be re-bagged when sold.

» Display mattresses should be put on a queen platform foundation.

» To keep your floor models looking great, you should swap them out as they begin to look worn (marked up, stained, squeaky foundations, etc.) To do this, simply sell the floor model and replace it with a new one.

» The desk with the computer and office phone is placed by the front door.

» Inventory is stored on the opposite wall of your mattress line-up. Keep the inventory in rows with a mattress/box as sets. Do not pancake stack your inventory, lean them up against the wall.

» NO foot protectors & NO pillows because we do not want to look like a store. We are only showing samples of what we have left in inventory.

"Action is the real measure of intelligence."

NAPOLEON HILL

(The legendary best-selling author of the number one most read self-help book of all-time.)

"Every adversity, every failure, every heartache carries with it the seed of an equal or greater benefit.."

NAPOLEON HILL

(The legendary best-selling author of the number one most read self-help book of all-time.)

Showroom Set Up

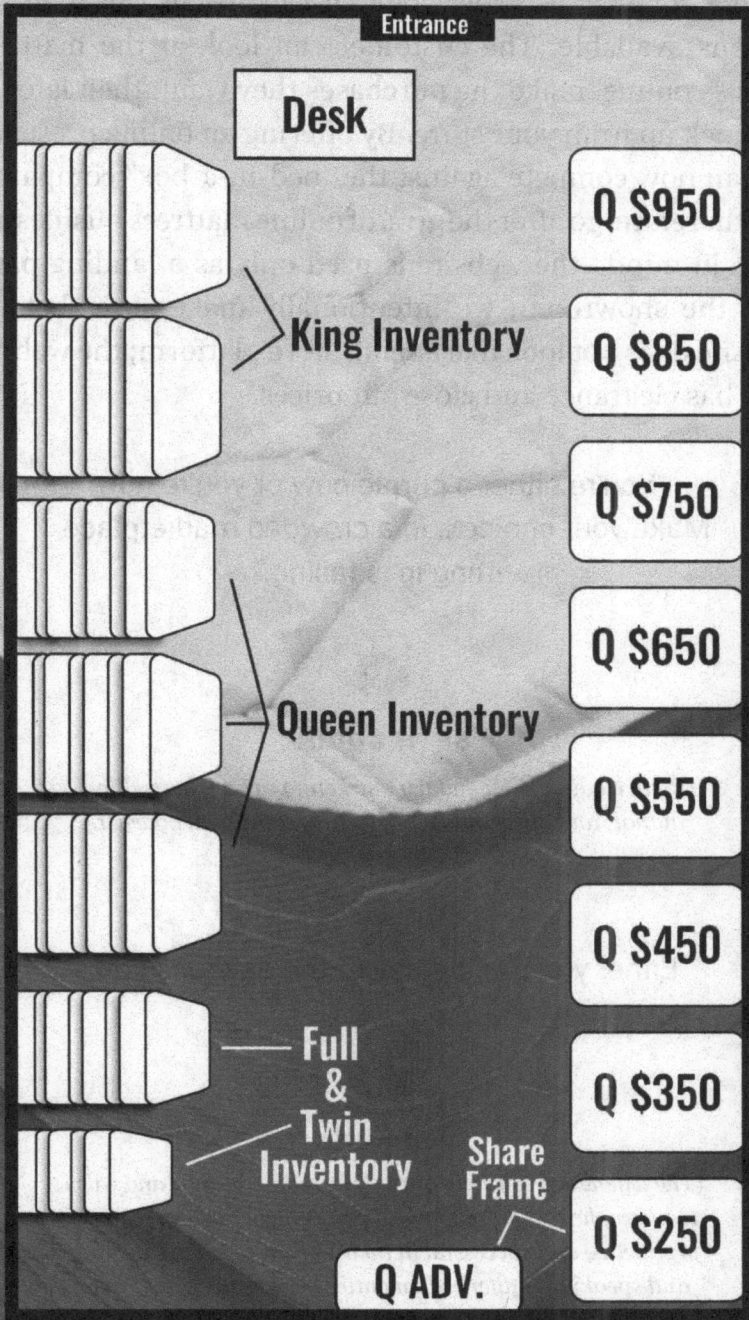

Entrance

Desk

King Inventory

Queen Inventory

Full
&
Twin
Inventory

Share
Frame

Q ADV.

Q $950

Q $850

Q $750

Q $650

Q $550

Q $450

Q $350

Q $250

Website Creation

As a company, we have created a local online ordering system for you to show your customers all the mattress options available. The customer can look at the mattress choices online, make the purchases they want, then later go and pick up from your store. By offering an online presence, we can now compete against the "bed-in-a-box" companies and therefore, go after the 30% of online mattress businesses. Keep in mind—the website is used only as a landing page. Like the showroom, we intentionally make sure that the website does not look like a retail store platform; the website only has clearance and close out prices.

"You're either a purple cow or you're not. Make your choice... in a crowded marketplace, fitting in is failing."

SETH GODIN

(Seth Godin is a legendary marketing expert, bestselling author, and guest on the ThrivetimeShow.com podcast.)

"Either you run the day or the day runs you."

JIM ROHN

(The legendary self-help guru, best-selling author and sales trainer who taught millions of people how to become more productive and successful in their lives. Jim Rohn's writing and speaking influenced an entire generation of self-help authors and speaks.)

Social Platforms

Create social media pages— this includes a Facebook Business page and a Google Business page. When creating these pages, it is very important to keep all your social platforms consistent with the look of the showroom. We want to keep the sense of urgency and emphasize the value. Remember, we are not a typical mattress store. We sell closeouts, clearance, and overstock items, and we are available by appointment only.

"Simple can be harder than complex: You have to work hard to get your thinking clean to make it simple. But it's worth it in the end because once you get there, you can move mountains."

STEVE JOBS

(The man who revolutionized the personal computer, recorded audio, telecommunications and animated movie industries. Steve Jobs co-founded Apple, turned around PIXAR while serving as their CEO and founded a company called NeXT which created an operating system that was later acquired by Apple.)

FREQUENTLY ASKED QUESTIONS:

What Type of Commercial Location Are You Looking For?

Finding Space— Darren Conrad's proven method for building a successful mattress business involves securing an empty rectangle 1,000-2,000 square-foot commercial space. As the owner of a mattress store you want to find a location somewhere that is close to your home. You want to secure a commercial space for your business that is easy to find and within a safe part of time (Neighborhood). In order for your business to be viable you must be able to receive deliveries from a fifty-three foot truck must repeatedly throughout the week.

What Is the First Step You Must Take to Find the Ideal Location for Your Business?

Remember, we are a destination location, not a retail store, so it doesn't really matter if your commercial space is located near high traffic streets or not. The first step you must take in order to find the ideal commercial space for your mattress business involves you driving around and searching for business parks, strip malls, industrial parks and empty retail space off of the main street. You want to choose locations that are safe to go to after dark.

What Do You Do After You Have Found An Ideal Location?

Contact the listing commercial realtor and let them know what you are looking for, and ask them if they can suggest other properties. Remember, commercial brokers and commercial real estate agents earn a commission by helping great people like you to find commercial space Commercial real estate agents are going earn a nice commission if they help you find an ideal commercial location for your business!

What If You Struggle to Find a Location By Driving Around?

If you are struggling to find a space while driving around go onto Google and type in the name of your city plus the keyword "commercial retail warehouse space for lease." Once you start searching on Google for "retail/warehouse space for rent" you will run into third party websites like Loopnet. com (and other third party websites). Loopnet.com is a great resource for finding space too, however it does not include private owners that are renting space. Do not rely solely on third party websites and commercial real estate agents to find space for you, YOU MUST SIMULTANEOUSLY CONTINUE TO SEARCH ON YOUR OWN UNTIL YOU HAVE FOUND A VIABLE PHYSICAL LOCATION FOR YOUR BUSINESS.

What Is the Ideal Price to Pay for the Commercial Space That You Are Renting?

Remember, as an entrepreneur it is not about how much money you make, it's about how much money you keep. Thus you want to keep your monthly lease expense as low as possible ($10-$15 per square foot is ideal). Once you find potential space, Darren Conrad and his team can help you negotiate the lease.

Why Is Finding Your Commercial Space Such An Important Step?

Finding an ideal commercial space for your business is VERY IMPORTANT. This step is arguably the most important in the process of opening up your mattress business for many reasons. The first being the most obvious; you need a showroom for customers to meet you at and view your inventory. Without a showroom for your product, you cannot sell any mattresses. Additionally, a physical showroom location is 100% necessary to obtain a Google Map. A Google Map is a crucial aspect of building a successful mattress business that gets found by your ideal and likely buyers (aka producing leads), and thus, drives revenue. Verifying your business on Google (having a Google Map) is a non-negotiable aspect in building a successful business of any kind.

Website Creation

As a company, we have created a POWERFUL local online ordering system for you to show your customers all the mattress options available. The customer can look at the mattress choices online, make the purchases they want, then later go and pick up from your store. By offering an online presence, we can now compete against the "bed-in-a-box" companies and therefore, go after the 30% of online mattress businesses. You must keep in mind that the website is used only as a landing page. Like the showroom, we intentionally make sure that the website does not look like a retail store platform; the website only has clearance and close out prices listed.

DEEP THOUGHTS FROM THE MATTRESS KING

❝❞

People that say it can't be done are usually getting interrupted by other people doing it.

—— Darren Conrad ——

CHAPTER 3

ADVERTISING
(WHEN YOU SNOOZE, YOU LOSE)

*THE GOAL IS TO WAKE UP
THE MARKETPLACE, TO GET
THEIR ATTENTION, AND TO GET
CONTACTS.*

**One out of ten people are in the market for a
new mattress. Let everyone know what you do!**

The more advertising sources you have, the better
chances you have of getting more contacts—Google,
Facebook Business page, Facebook Marketplace, Craigslist,
newspapers' online classifieds, flyers, road signs, business
cards, etc. Spend time each and every day reviewing and
placing ads. In order to maximize your advertising, check
out the following three pieces of advice—lowest prices,
be positioned to be the first ad seen, and create a sense of
urgency.

Lowest Prices

The first thing that you need is to have the lowest prices in
the market. This requires advertising an item for sale that is
below our cost, but remember the goal is to generate contacts.
I'm not suggesting that we advertise free mattresses, but
the lowest price will generate the most contacts. The secret
to dominating in your market is not being afraid to price a
low price. This is so important, remember the goal is to get

contacts. Do not focus on making a profit on the advertised mattress. Stay focused on getting massive amounts of contacts and clearing out your weekly inventory. The profit will be there if you stay focused on driving contacts.

To illustrate this point, I once had a competitor try to harm my business. He posted an ad on Facebook Marketplace—it said "Free Mattresses," and he put my phone number as the contact. My phone rang off the hook, and I answered each call and shared my full approach with each and every person as I normally would. Through that process, I sold A LOT of mattresses! After that happened, I thought to myself, "Why would my competitor direct people who are in the market for mattresses to contact me?" What he thought would be damaging to me and my business was actually a huge benefit for me as well as a great learning experience. He did not know that when people are in the market, they're usually only in the market for 3 to 5 days, and on top of that, they usually only shop at 1.6 places before making a purchase. That means if they contact me first, this puts me in a huge advantage! I can be the first to share my story with them, my sales pitch, and the value that I have in mattresses.

Get Your Ad Seen First

The second thing that you need is to be positioned first so that your ad is seen before your competition's ads. Whether it's on Facebook Marketplace, Google, Craigslist, or any platform, your ad should always be the first.

Sense of Urgency

The third thing you need to have is a sense of urgency. We always write our ads with a sense of urgency with the language we use. For writing the ad, make sure to be creative. Write ads that look and feel like you're going out of business, but don't actually say that you're going out of business. Write ads as if you are selling your own personal mattress, and make it look like you're selling one item only. Use verbiage like, "must go," "clearing out," and "liquidating." NO emoji's, NO stickers, NO stock photos, NO graphics and never advertise sale promotions.

Here's the four core advertisement examples:

1. King Size Mattress Must Sell, Still in Original Plastic, Willing to Sacrifice $200.

2. Queen Pillowtop Mattress for Sale, Excellent Condition, Willing to Let Go for $150.

3. Full Mattress Set, Still Boxed $140.

4. Clearing out Overstock & Closeout Mattresses:
   King $200
   Queen $125
   Full $100
   While supply lasts!

Brand New Mattresses.. Must Go!
$69 · In stock

Message

Details

Condition   New

I'm clearing out brand new mattresses, direct from the manufacturers.

First Come First Served!
Twins from $69
Fulls from $89
Queens from $99
Kings from $199

Cash, Card and Payment Plans

Send seller a message

Good afternoon, is this still available?

Send

#!WE CAN'T WAIT TO MEET YA!# MATTRESS CLEAROUTS!! 50%-80% OFF!! GOING FAST!! 1ST COME 1ST SERVE!!
Pillowtops, Memory Foam, Plush, Firm, Gel, Adjustable Beds and more. Clearing out OVERSTOCK Inventory from a National Mattress Distributor. Everything is new in plastic and marked down 50%-80% OFF what you would pay for in a store. Starting at $130-Twins, $140-Fulls, $150-Queens, $300-Kings, $575-Cal Kings. Cash, Credit, Debit and 90 days same as cash, no credit check financing. Call, text or message Laurie at (209) 327-0443. Delivery is available. Family Owned & Operated!!

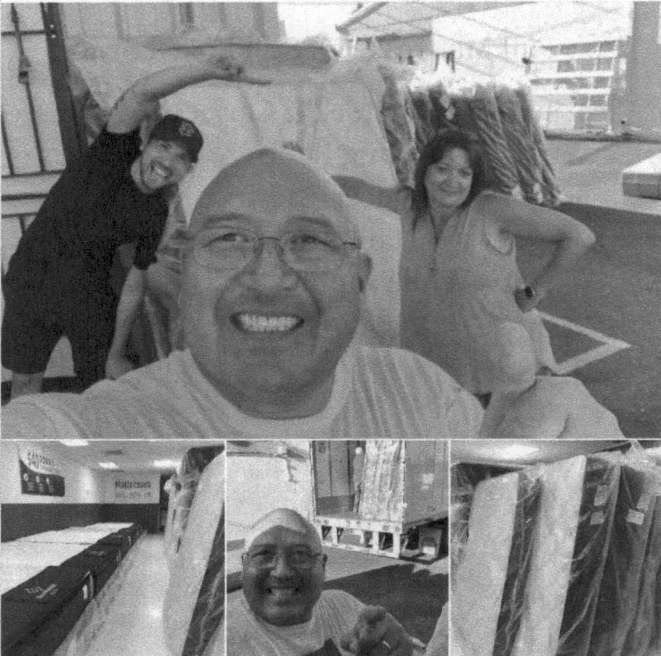

With these type of ads, the customer will call and ask, "Is this still available?" If that is what you're hearing from customers, then your ad is working. If people are contacting you and saying, "What are your hours?," then that means your ads look more like a retail store, which is not what we want. We want individual ads and clearance ads that have a sense of urgency.

To determine the price to advertise, spend at least 15 minutes every day scanning your competition's ads. Search Mattress Queen/King/Full Size price on FB Marketplace. Whatever the price our competitor has listed, we will advertise $10 less. If our competitor uses an ad that offers financing from any finance company, we will use a similar ad with a lower price in addition to our regular ads.

Google Page: BREAKING NEWS!!! This just in!!! Humans are using Google to search for the products and services they are looking to buy and thus you must be relevant in the Google search engine results. In order to be relevant and to SHOW UP in the Google search results, you must have an optimized Google Map list! Why do you need to have an optimized Google Map listing? Because you don't hate money and you want your customers to find you when they are looking for a mattress store in your local area.

Google Reviews are a great way to build trust and credibility, improve local search rankings, and increase sales. They act as social proof, influencing customers who search reviews before making a purchase.

Steps To create a Google Business Profile:

Step 1: Sign in or create a Google account

- Go to <u>business.google.com</u> and sign in
- If you don't have a Google account, you can create one for free at google.com/accounts.
- Click the blue "Add Business" button
- Click "Add Single Business"

Step 2: Add your business information

- Enter your business name and choose the most accurate category that describes your business.
    - The Name of the Google Map Must Match the Name of the LLC (Limited Liability Corporation) or DBA (Doing Business As) Exactly.
- Location: Specify the physical location you have that customers can visit.
- Contact Information: Add your phone number and website.
- Service Areas: Select all surrounding cities within 25 minute radius of the business.

Step 3: Complete your profile

- Add details like your operating hours, business description, photos and link social profiles.
    - Write Original Business Description (750 Characters)
    - Do not include marketing slogans in Business Description
- You can also add information about your services, and attributes like whether the business is women-led.

Step 4: Verify your business

- You will need to verify your listing before it can become visible to customers.

- In order to get verified, office must be setup with:

  - A desk, computer that is connected to power, monitors connected to computer, mouse, keyboard, office phone, chair, and wall art.

  - A sign on the door that includes your business name, phone number, web address, business hours and physical address.

- Follow the on-screen instructions to complete the verification process, which may include options like a postcard by mail, video verification or office photo verification.

Step 5: Manage your profile

Once verified, you can manage your profile to keep it up to date, respond to reviews, and post updates, offers, and events.

- **V**ideo Reviews

- **I**mages

- **S**earch Engine Content

- **M**ore Google Reviews

Facebook Business Page: To sell on Facebook Marketplace for your business, create a Facebook Business Page and use Marketplace to create new listings. When listing, use high-quality photos, competitive pricing, and consider using paid ads to extend your reach. Post clearance advertisements on the page and boost it weekly. Spend $50-$100 a day continually. Open 24/7 with just your phone number.

To create a listing:

- Find the listing tool: Go to the Marketplace icon and click "Create New Listing."

- Add product details: Include a compelling title, high-quality photos (up to 10), a detailed description, competitive price, and relevant tags or categories.

SAMPLE AD BELOW

MASSIVE CLEAROUTS!! GOING VERY FAST!!
DON'T MISS OUT!! 1ST COME 1ST SERVE!!
Pillowtops, Memory Foam, Plush, Firm, Gel, Adjustable Beds and more. Clearing out
OVERSTOCK Inventory from a National Mattress Distributor. Everything is new in plastic and
marked down 50%-80% OFF what you would pay for in a store. Starting at $130-Twins, $140-
Fulls, $150-Queens, $300-Kings, $575-Cal Kings. Cash, Credit, Debit and 90 days same as
cash, no credit check financing. Call, text or message   . Delivery is
available. Family owned and operated!

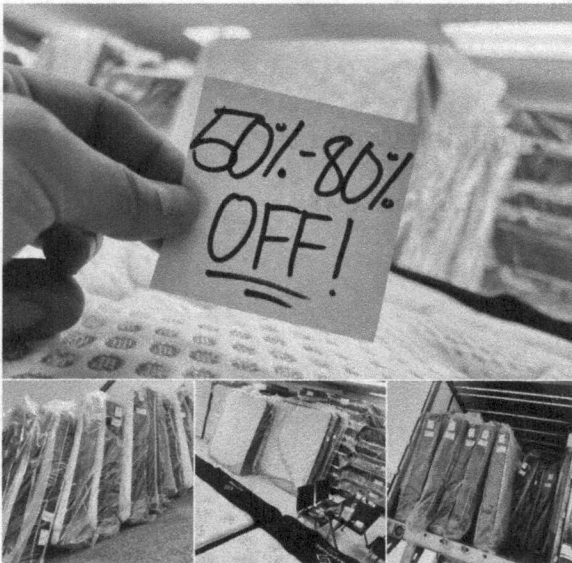

Facebook Marketplace / Online Classified / Craigslist Ads: These types of ads can be posted daily, and we suggest doing 8 of these ads every day (Additionally, you can pay for a FB posting service).

For photos, make sure to use your own photos of ONE item from inventory, NO store photos. Always avoid looking like a store. Additionally, do not use stock photos, icons, or any highlighting. Take all of the photos yourself and don't use other people's photos.

For pricing, I dominate advertising by not being afraid to lower my price. Remember—the lowest price gets the most contacts!

$150
Queen Size Mattress! Ok
Oklahoma City, OK

$399
New sealy Mattresses. Queen $399. King $499. Delivery available
Oklahoma City, OK

$158
Almost Free!! Need to sell these beds and mattresses. With free delivery within 4...
Noble, OK

$120 $150
Barely Used Queen Pillowtop Matress
Oklahoma City, OK

$78
Moving Out Sale ||| Queen Mattress with Box Spring For Sale with Free Delivery
Oklahoma City, OK

$125
Queen mattress
Nichols Hills, OK

Facebook Groups: Search Buy Sell in Groups on Facebook. Join as many local groups and post ads weekly. Read & FOLLOW the rules in each group before posting. Post the clearance ad & individual K/Q add in ten groups every day.

Buy and Sell Orange Park-Jacksonville
Public · 44K members · 90+ posts a day
92 friends are members
Join

Buy, Sell, or Trade ANYTHING!
Public · 17K members · 90+ posts a day
42 friends are members
Join

Atlantic/Neptune Beach Buy/Sell/Offer up.
Public · 39K members · 90+ posts a day
258 friends are members
Join

★Jacksonville And St. Johns Buy~Sell & Trade★
Private · 21K members · 90+ posts a day
Join

Marketplace ☑ Buy & Sell Anything Near Me - Facebook Local Marketplace
Public · 236K members · 90+ posts a day
2 friends are members
Join

TRADE/BUY/SELL Flagler/ St. johns/ St. Augustine area
Public · 12K members · 90+ posts a day
25 friends are members
Join

Jacksonville Man Cave Marketplace – Buy, Sell & Swap
Private · 43K members · 90+ posts a day
Join

Marketplace Items For Sale Local By Owner: Buy and Sell Used Items On FB
Public · 160K members · 40+ posts a day
5 friends are members
Join

Buy Sell Florida
Public · 55K members · 90+ posts a day
8 friends are members
Join

"Half of the battle is selling music, not singing it."

ROD STEWART

(The legendary British singer and songwriter with the distinctive raspy voice whose career spanned five decades and who sold 120 million records worldwide.)

Flyers: The purpose is to get CONTACTS. We can put flyers in gyms, grocery stores, coffee shops, college campuses, laundry mats, or anywhere else you can think of.

FOR SALE

QUEEN SIZE MATTRESS

Still in original package.

$100.00

Text (614) 222-1234

Queen Mattress (614) 222-1234	Queen Mattress (614) 222-1234	Queen Mattress (614) 222-1234	Queen Mattress (614) 222-1234	Queen Mattress (614) 222-1234	Queen Mattress (614) 222-1234	Queen Mattress (614) 222-1234	Queen Mattress (614) 222-1234	Queen Mattress (614) 222-1234	Queen Mattress (614) 222-1234

Road Signs: Hand written on 18x24 white corrugated plastic with step stakes. We advertise Queen or King ONLY.

For Sale

QUEEN MATTRESS

NEW $100

Call/Text

(904) 870-0509

Business Cards: Have these with you at all times; they are like miniature road signs. You can distribute these at hair salons, gyms, crossfit, yoga studios, Starbucks, chiropractors, restaurants, etc.

Local Mattress Clearance Center
King Mattress $200
Queen Mattress $100

Darren Conrad
Owner

AmericaBeddingDirect.com
(904) 307-1765

"Concentrate all your thoughts upon the work in hand. The sun's rays do not burn until brought to a focus."

ALEXANDER GRAHAM BELL

(The inventor of the first practical telephone and the co-founder of AT&T, American Telephone and Telegraph Company.)

The Biblical Ten Commandments
(Found In Exodus Chapter 20: 3-17):

Commandment #1 - [3] Thou shalt have no other gods before me. [4] Thou shalt not make unto thee any graven image, or any likeness of any thing that is in heaven above, or that is in the earth beneath, or that is in the water under the earth. [5] Thou shalt not bow down thyself to them, nor serve them: for I the Lord thy God am a jealous God, visiting the iniquity of the fathers upon the children unto the third and fourth generation of them that hate me; [6] And shewing mercy unto thousands of them that love me, and keep my commandments.

Commandment #2 - [7] Thou shalt not take the name of the Lord thy God in vain; for the Lord will not hold him guiltless that taketh his name in vain.

Commandment #3 - [8] Remember the sabbath day, to keep it holy.

Commandment #4 - [9] Six days shalt thou labour, and do all thy work: [10] But the seventh day is the sabbath of the Lord thy God: in it thou shalt not do any work, thou, nor thy son, nor thy daughter, thy manservant, nor thy maidservant, nor thy cattle, nor thy stranger that is within thy gates: [11] For in six days the Lord made heaven and earth, the sea, and all that in them is, and rested the seventh day: wherefore the Lord blessed the sabbath day, and hallowed it.

Commandment #5 - [12] Honour thy father and thy mother: that thy days may be long upon the land which the Lord thy God giveth thee.

Commandment #6 - [13] Thou shalt not kill.

Commandment #7 - [14] Thou shalt not commit adultery.

Commandment #8 - [15] Thou shalt not steal.

Commandment #9 - [16] Thou shalt not bear false witness against thy neighbour.

Commandment #10 - [17] Thou shalt not covet thy neighbour's house, thou shalt not covet thy neighbour's wife, nor his manservant, nor his maidservant, nor his ox, nor his ass, nor any thing that is thy neighbour's.

The American Bedding Direct 10 Commandments for Achieving Success:

Commandment #1 - Thou shall take responsibility for the success or failure of your business.

Commandment #2 - Thou shall urgently secure a commercial location for your business.

Commandment #3 - Thou shall urgently register a Google Map within your local designated market area.

Commandment #4 - Thou shall gather two times more objective Google reviews than any of the local mattress business competitors within your designated market area.

Commandment #5 - Thou shall diligently meet with your business coach each week to learn what action items you need to take to earn the money you want to make.

Commandment #6 - Thou shall block out the time needed to turn your to-do list into a to-done list.

Commandment #7 - Thou shall gather two times more objective Google reviews than any of the local mattress business competitors within your designated market area.

Commandment #8 - Thou shall measure what you treasure and track where you don't want your business to slack.

Commandment #9 - Thou shall call, text and email your leads until they cry, buy or die.

Commandment #10 - Thou shall gather two times more objective Google reviews than any of the local mattress business competitors within your designated market area.

LOCK YOURSELF INTO THE WAGE CAGE.

SINCE WHEN DO WE HIRE ZOMBIES?

OH, BOB! HE'S BEEN THAT WAY SINCE '93 WHEN HE GAVE UP ON HIS DREAMS.

HANG IN THERE

"SOME PEOPLE DIE AT 25 AND AREN'T BURIED UNTIL 75."
- BENJAMIN FRANKLIN

In order for you to achieve total SEARCH ENGINE DOMINATION and DRAMATICALLY increase your level of COMPENSATION, you must simply check off and complete all of the checklist items on this website evaluation. We humbly refer to this checklist as "The Ultimate Search Engine Domination Checklist."

Chapter 4: The Ultimate Search Engine

DOMINATION CHECKLIST

(AND WEBSITE EVALUATION):

_____ Host your website with a reliable hosting service. If your website is hosted with an unreliable hosting service, you will rank lower in the search engines. We recommend using GoDaddy.com. Don't host your website with some local, janky hosting provider who lives with his mom in the basement.

_____ Host your website with the fastest package that you can afford. Google REALLY CARES about how long it takes for your website to load. Why? Because people get impatient and will quickly move on to another website if your website takes too long to load. On January 17th of 2018, Google formally announced the "Speed Update." Google's plan called for them to slowly roll out the new search engine ranking criteria to give web-developers plenty of time to make their websites load much, much faster. To test the speed of your website, visit: https://developers.google.com/speed/pagespeed/insights/ To read more about Google's new speed requirements, visit: https://www.forbes.com/sites/jaysondemers/2018/01/29/will-googles-new-page-speed-criteria-affect-your-site/#396634ed6a8f

_____ Build your website on the WordPress platform. "WordPress offers the best out-of-the-box search engine optimization imaginable." - Tim Ferriss (Best-selling author of *The 4-Hour Work Week*, *The 4-Hour Body*, *The 4-Hour Chef*, *Tools of Titans*, and *Tribe of Mentors*. He is also an early stage investor in Facebook, Twitter, Evernote, Uber, etc.)

Don't use any other website building platform than WordPress. If you hire coders to custom build your website on PHP or .NET you will end up hating your life as a result of having a website that nobody can update other than the entitled, nefarious employees who now have the ability to hold you hostage. Trust us here. We have personally coached hundreds of clients and every time our coaching clients have a custom-built website, the business owner at some point has been held hostage by the employee who is the only person who knows how to update the custom built, non-search engine friendly, and ridiculously complicated website. Building your website on WordPress puts the power back in your hands as a business owner because you can update the website yourself if you have to.

PRO TIP: USE WORDPRESS.ORG NOT WORDPRESS.COM

Wordpress.org is the open source platform used to power the best SEO compliant websites in the world. Wordpress.com is their platform that does not allow for plugins or optimal website optimization.

*Avoid wordpress.com

_____ Build a mobile-friendly website. What is a mobile friendly website? Check your website's mobile compliance at: https://search.google.com/test/mobile-friendly. If this link changes in the future, just search for "Google mobile compliance test" in the Google search engine and you'll find it.

_____ Install HTTPS encryption onto your website. HTTPS encryption stands for Hypertext Transfer Protocol Secure. What does that mean? HTTPS encryption makes your website more difficult for bad people to hack, thus making it tougher for very bad people to crash your website and to use your website as a way to steal the personal information of your valuable clients and patrons. Google ranks websites higher who have invested the additional money needed to add HTTPS encryption to their website. How many times would you use Google if every time their search results sent you to websites that had been hacked into by cyber criminals and internet hackers?

← → C ⌂ 🔒 https://www.youtube.com

_____Install the Yoast.com search engine optimization plugin into your website. What is Yoast? Yoast SEO is the best WordPress plugin on the planet when it comes to search engine optimization. Yoast was built and designed in a way to make search engine optimization approachable for everyone, and thus we love Yoast. Yoast makes it possible for people who are not complete nerds to proactively manage the search engine optimization of their website.

What is a plugin?

A plugin is a piece of code or software that provides a variety of functions that you can add to your WordPress website. Plugins allow you to increase the functional capacity of your website without having to hire a bunch of nefarious, entitled custom coders who are typically hard to manage because you do not have any idea what they are working on or what they are talking about 90% of the time.

• •

\</\> _____Uniquely optimize every meta title tag on every page of your website. The title tag is simply a hypertext markup language (HTML) element on a website that specifies to search engines what a particular web page is all about. "According to Moz.com, the best practice for the title tag length is to keep titles under 70 characters." An example would be, "Full Package Media | Dallas Real Estate Photography | 972-885-8823."

Full Package Media | Dallas Real Estate Photography | 972-885-8823
https://fullpackagemedia.com/ ▾
Looking for the best in the business when it comes to Dallas Real Estate Photography? You need to

☰ _____Uniquely optimize every meta description on every page of your website. The meta description is simply part of the hypertext markup language (HTML) code that provides a brief summary about a web page. Search engines like Google usually show the meta description in search engine results. Don't make your meta descriptions more than 160 characters in length. An ample example would be, "Looking for the best in the business when it comes to Dallas Real Estate Photography? You need to call Full Package Media today at 972-885-8823."

Looking for the best in the business when it comes to Dallas Real Estate Photography? You need to call Full Package Media today at 972-885-8823.
Careers · About Us · Contact Us · Client Login

🔑 _____Uniquely optimize the keywords on every page of your website. Meta keywords are a very specific kind of meta tag that will show up in the hypertext markup language (HTML) code on web pages and these will tell the search engines what the web page is really all about. An example of specific keyword optimization would be "Berj Najarian." You may be thinking, who is Berj Najarian?

Berj Najarian serves as the New England Patriots Director of Football and the "Chief of Staff" for the legendary Coach Bill Belichick, who has won a total of 8 Super Bowl titles since beginning his coaching career in the National Football League. If someone is searching for "Berj Najarian," there is a high probability that they already know who "Berj Najarian" is, and if you want to rank high in the search engines when people are searching for "Berj Najarian" you definitely want to make sure that you have declared your meta keyword phrase as "Berj Najarian."

Quick Note: If at any point while reading this you are beginning to feel overwhelmed, just submit your website for an audit and deep dive evaluation and we'll do the heavy lifting for you. You can submit your website to be audited at: www.ThriveTimeShow.com/Website

_____ Create 1,000 words of original, non-AI-generated content and relevant text (content) per page on your website. Are we saying that somebody actually has to write 1,000 original words of original and relevant text for every page of your website? Yes. Isn't there a hack? NO. Can't there be a better way? No. Can't you just go out and hire a company out of India to use "spinners" to slightly change existing text for you? NO. Can't you just copy content from another website? NO. You can spend every minute of every day trying to find some blogger or some website experts out there who will tell you that someone on your team doesn't need to invest the time needed to create 1,000 words of both original and relevant content, and you will eventually find them, and they will be 100% wrong. However, they will gladly take your money. YOU OR A MEMBER OF YOUR TEAM MUST WRITE 1,000 WORDS OF BOTH ORIGINAL AND RELEVANT CONTENT FOR EVERY PAGE OF YOUR WEBSITE.

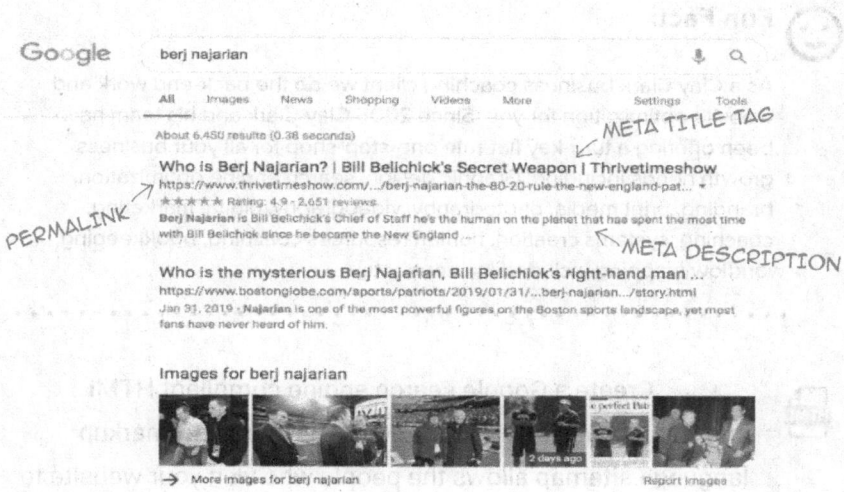

XML _____ Create a Google search engine compliant .XML sitemap on your website. What is an .XML sitemap? XML stands for Extensible Markup Language. A quality XML sitemap serves as a map of your website, which allows the Google search engine to find all of the important pages located within your website. As a website owner, unless you hate money, you REALLY WANT GOOGLE to be able to crawl (find, rank, and sort) all of the important pages on your website. Yoast.com has tools that will actually generate Google compliant .XML sitemaps for you. Don't worry, you can do this!

😊 **Fun Fact:**

I had to take Algebra 3 times en route to getting into Oral Roberts university and I was eventually kicked out of college for writing a parody about the school's president "ORU Slim Shady," which you can currently find on YouTube. If I can learn and master search engine optimization, you can too!

😊 **Fun Fact:**

As a Clay Clark business coaching client we do the back-end work and website optimization for you. Since 2006 Clay Clark and his team have been offering a turn-key flat-rate one-stop-shop for all your business growth needs including: Graphic design, search engine optimization, branding, print media, photography, videography, digital marketing, coaching, systems creation, human resources coaching, bookkeeping, workflow mapping included (no contracts).

. . . .

🗎 _____Create a Google search engine compliant HTML sitemap. What's an HTML site map? A hypertext markup language sitemap allows the people who visit your website to easily navigate your website. This sitemap should be located at the bottom of your website and should be labeled as a "Sitemap."

Hiding your sitemap for any reason is a bad idea because Google assumes that if you are hiding your sitemap you are probably trying to hide something. Don't change the background of your website to be the same color as your sitemap's font or do anything tricky here. You want to make sure that your website's sitemap can easily be found at the bottom of your website. See the example below:

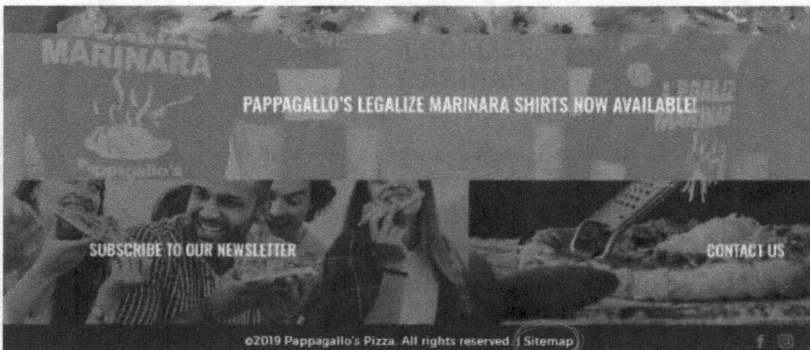

_____Create a clickable phone number. If you ever want to sell something to humans on the planet Earth you must make your contact information easy to find. Thus, you want to make your phone number easily available to find at either the top right or at the bottom of your website. When coaching your web-developer, force them to make your phone number a "click-to-call" phone number so that users on your website who are using a mobile phone (almost everyone) can simply click the number to call you. In our shameless attempt to make this the BEST, MOST HUMBLE, and ACTIONABLE SEARCH ENGINE OPTIMIZATION book of all time, we have provided the following real examples from REAL clients just like you who we have really helped to REALLY increase their REAL sales year after year:

☺ **Fun Fact:**

As a Clay Clark business coaching client we do the back-end work and website optimization for you. Since 2006 Clay Clark and his team have been offering a turn-key flat-rate one-stop-shop for all your business growth needs including: Graphic design, search engine optimization, branding, print media, photography, videography, digital marketing, coaching, systems creation, human resources coaching, bookkeeping, workflow mapping included (no contracts).

● ●

🎗 _____Have a Social Proof. If you don't hate money and you are not a committed socialist, you will want to include some social proof near the top of your website. What is social proof? "Social proof" is a phrase and a term that was originally created by the best-selling author, Robert Cialdini, in his book *Influence*. The best social proof examples are:

a. Real testimonials from real, current and former clients are super powerful.

b. Media features and appearances on credible media sources like Bloomberg, Fox Business, Entrepreneur. com, Fast Company, etc.

c. Proudly showing that you have earned the highest and most reviews in your local business niche.

100

d. Celebrity endorsements from celebrities that have earned the trust of your ideal and likely buyers.

e. Listed below is an example that will showcase to you what it looks like to use social proof effectively.

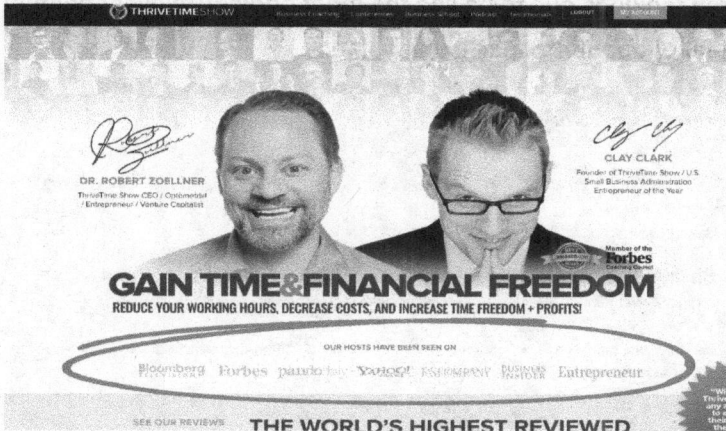

_____Make the logo return to home. Allow the logo on your website to serve as your "homepage" button. As of 2019, most people assume that if they click your logo they are going to be taken back to the homepage of your website.

_____Create original content. You must create more original and relevant content than anyone else in the world about your specific search engine focus. If you want to come up top in the world for the phrase "organic supplements," you must then create the most original and relevant content on the planet about "organic supplements." If you want to come up top in your city for the phrase "knee pain Tulsa," then you must what? You must create the most original and relevant content on the planet about "knee pain Tulsa."

If you want to come up top in the search engine results for the phrase "America's #1 business coach," then you must create the most original and relevant content on the planet about "America's #1 business coach." Listed below are a few examples of receiving high search rankings due to having the most original, relevant content on the planet about that particular subject.

america's #1 business coach

All   News   Images   Videos   Maps   More   Settings   Tools

About 5,670,000 results (0.35 seconds)

Business Coach | Bill Belichick's #1 Fan and America's #1 Business ...
https://www.thrivetimeshow.com/the...show/business-coach-management-principles/
★★★★★ Rating: 99% · 2,651 votes
Bill Belichick's number one fan and America's #1 business coach Clay Clark teaches many of the successful management principles that Belichick ...

People also ask

Who is the best business coach in the world?   ⌄

The Little Gym of SE Tulsa
4.7 ★★★★★ (14) · Gymnastics center
3.3 mi · 6556 E 91st St · (918) 492-2626
Open · Closes 7:30PM   WEBSITE   DIRECTIONS
Their website mentions gymnastics classes

Twist & Shout Tumbling & Cheer
3.6 ★★★★☆ (8) · Gym
6.2 mi · 4820 S 83rd E Ave · (918) 622-5867
Closed · Opens 5PM   WEBSITE   DIRECTIONS
Their website mentions tumbling classes

≡ More places

Tumbling Tulsa | Tulsa Tumbling Lessons | 918-764-8804
https://justicetumblingco.com/
If you are looking for the best and highest reviewed tumbling Tulsa place, you need to call us at Justice Tumbling today and see what makes us better.
Services · About · Schedule · Testimonials

Tulsa Cheerleading | Tumbling Tulsa | Tulsa Tumbling | 918-986-5785
https://tumblesmart.com/
Tulsa's Most Reviewed Tumbling Program. Tumble Smart Athletics. Free Evaluation LessonMeet the Owner. Tumbling Tulsa Gymnast Stars. Experience the ...
Classes · Facility · About · Testimonials

Google   tulsa knee pain

Tulsa Knee Pain - Revolution Health Tulsa
https://www.revolutionhealth.org/.../tulsa-knee-pain-revolution-health-is-bring-in-a-re... ▾
Find the best treatment for your **Tulsa knee pain** right here in Tulsa. Find out more about Revolution Health by calling at 918-935-3636.

Tulsa knee Pain | Revolution Health Oklahoma
https://www.revolutionhealth.org/.../tulsa-knee-pain-find-the-top-and-quickest-result-f... ▾
The best prolotherapy is right here at Revolution Health for **Tulsa knee pain**.

Best Prolotherapy Treatments Tulsa | Tulsa Knee Pain
https://www.revolutionhealth.org/.../tulsa-knee-pain-find-the-best-possible-tulsa-knee-... ▾
Best of the Best Prolotherapy Treatments for your **tulsa knee Pain**.

Non-invasive remedies relieve knee pain without surgery - Tulsa World
https://www.tulsaworld.com/...knee-pain.../article_6bdf681d-d017-554c-9ecc-fae529... ▾
Mar 13, 2019 - Dear Doctor K: I have osteoarthritis of the knee. Are there ways to relieve my knee pain without drugs or surgery?

💬 _____Create a "Testimonials," "Case Studies," or a "Success Stories" portion of your website if you want to sell something to humans who were not born yesterday. Most shoppers today have become savvy and are aware of the fact that great companies generate great reviews (and occasionally bad ones) and that bad companies chronically generate bad reviews (and occasionally some good ones). Thus, most people will want to actually see testimonials, case studies or success stories from real clients that have actually worked with your company in the past.

In fact, not having testimonials, case studies and success stories on your website freaks most people out to the point that they won't even call you or fill out your contact form.

How do we know this? Well, for starters, we are humans who also happen to be consumers, and Forbes tells us that, "Almost 90% of consumers said they read reviews for local businesses. In other words, if you are not investing efforts into online reputation management, then you are missing out on having control of the first impression your business has." - Online Reviews and Their Impact On the Bottom Line by Matt Bowman - https://www.forbes.com/sites/forbesagencycouncil/2019/01/15/online-reviews-and-their-impact-on-the-bottom-line/#35d3b4955bde

☺ **Fun Fact:**

As a Clay Clark business coaching client we do the back-end work and website optimization for you. Since 2006 Clay Clark and his team have been offering a turn-key flat-rate one-stop-shop for all your business growth needs including: Graphic design, search engine optimization, branding, print media, photography, videography, digital marketing, coaching, systems creation, human resources coaching, bookkeeping, workflow mapping included (no contracts).

• •

"Perfectionism is often an excuse for procrastination."

- PAUL GRAHAM

(The entrepreneur investor, incubator, and coach behind AirBNB, Dropbox, and Reddit)

▶ _____Include a compelling 60-second video / commercial (on the top portion above the fold) on your website to improve your conversion rate. To provide you with an ample example of clients that we have personally worked with who have used a "website header video" in route to dramatically increasing their sales, check out:

VIDEO PLAY BUTTON

_____Create a "top of the website" call to action that your ideal and likely buyers will relate to and connect with. You want to make it SUPER EASY for your ideal and likely buyers to call you, to schedule an appointment with you, or for them to do business with you in the most convenient way possible. As an AMPLE EXAMPLE, check out EITRLounge.com and OXIFresh. com:

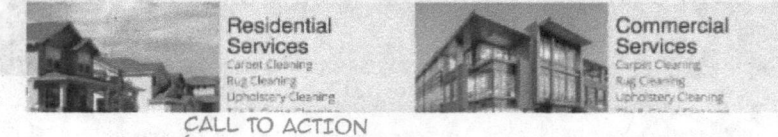

_____ Create a "No-Brainer" sales offer deal that is so GOOD, so HOT, and so IRRESISTIBLE that your ideal and likely buyers simply cannot resist the urge to at least try out your services and products. As an example, we would encourage you to check out the following websites.

Introduction: The SEO Manifesto

If you are a human on the planet earth, there is a good chance that you have used the internet to search for products and services you need or want. In fact, nearly every human I have met uses their smart phone to search for the products and services they need and want. Former Vice President Al Gore (the man who once claimed to have invented the Internet) has one. People are now officially using the Internet to shop. Thus, I would like to ask you three questions:

» *How much would it be worth to you for your business to be at the top of search results displayed by Google?*

» *How much is it costing you to not be at the top of Google search engine results?*

» *What terms are your ideal and likely buyers typing into the Google search bar on a daily basis to find the products and services that most closely relate to what your company offers?*

If you don't know the answers to these three questions, don't freak out, but also, don't move on without e-mailing us at info@ThriveTimeShow.com so that we can coach you through finding the answers to these questions.

Now, you might be a motivated and loyal Microsoft employee or a Yahoo employee and you might be saying to yourself, "But what if I use Bing or Yahoo and not Google as my search engine?" Don't stress, the game-changing systems I'm about to teach you will help you climb to the top of search engine results, regardless of which search engine your ideal and likely buyers are using. To get a baseline audit of your website so that you can quickly determine what you are doing right and wrong, just request a free website audit by e-mailing us at info@ThriveTimeShow.com.

I promise that you have the mental capacity to learn this. We've worked with and personally coached thousands of busy business owners like you and in every case, we have been able to teach anyone who is sincerely motivated to learn how to dominate search engine results. We know that search engine optimization is currently one of the most affordable, proven, and powerful marketing strategies available, and we believe it to be a huge issue if you do not know how search engine optimization (commonly referred to as SEO) truly works. Search engine optimization should not be viewed as mysterious or overwhelming. It should be seen as just another core daily task that is executed by your business every day, just like turning the lights on and opening the door. Up to now, you probably have not learned the dark arts of search engine optimization because...

> » You have denied that your ideal and likely buyers actually use the internet to find both the products and services they are looking for.

> » You have read too many search engine optimization blogs and have been falsely led to believe that the internet is too complicated and that Google is always changing, so even attempting to optimize your website is a waste of time.

> » You have yet to discover a system for search engine optimization that is both clear and understandable.

To create the system that we are going to teach you today, please know that we first experimented on ourselves (members of our team are owners and partners in dozens of businesses). We then successfully taught this system and coached hundreds of clients through this process. Our team painstakingly invested thousands of hours into the creation of these effective search engine techniques, and have read countless best-practice search engine optimization books on the subject to create what is THE BEST SEARCH ENGINE OPTIMIZATION SYSTEM ON THE PLANET. If you would like to read more on the subject of search engine optimization, we highly recommend that you read the following books:

» **Get Rich Click** – by Mark Ostrofsky – This book is endorsed by Steve Wozniak who co-founded that little company called Apple.

» **Search Optimization All-in-One** – by Bruce Clay – This book is very detailed and has the potential to blow your mind...so be careful.

» **Honest Seduction: Using Post-Click Marketing to Turn Landing Pages into Game-Changers** – by Scott Brinker, Anna Talerico and Justin Talerico.

After you finish reading the 1,500 pages of these books about how to harness the power of internet marketing, you will be a certified nerd and we will give you a high-five when you see us in person at a Thrive15.com workshop. Once you know what the heck you are doing, you must then commit to being a diligent doer and not a happy hoper. You must commit to taking the action steps that are required to win because knowledge is only potential power.

> "Knowledge is not power; it is only potential power that becomes real through use."
>
> *– Napoleon Hill*
> **(Bestselling author for whom the founder of Thrive15.com, Clay Clark, named his son...Aubrey Napoleon-Hill Clark)**

Getting to the top of search engine results is not an overnight process that will immediately begin sending your business life-changing amounts of inbound leads from your website. However, I promise that if you follow these checklists that we are providing and our proven search engine optimization rules, you will rise to page one in Google search results. Let's do this.

The Google Domination Equation

Proper Google Website Architecture (must follow Google's canonical rules) + Proper Google Mobile Compliance + Reviews + Most Relevant Original Content + Most High Quality Backlinks = Top of Google Search Engine Results

⊞ **Architecture** + ☐ **Mobile** + ✦ **Reviews**
📑 **Content** + ⬦ **Backlinks** = **Google Domination**

My friend, the bottom line is that the sites that have the most overall Google compliant architecture, the most mobile compliant architecture, the most original relevant content and the most backlinks, win. Once you wrap your mind around this idea, you can win. However, before you can win, you must first know what search terms (also referred to as "keyword phrases") are actually winnable. As an example, let's say you want to come up to the top of the Google search results for the word search term, "San Diego bakery." To show you if this search term is actually winnable, I'll walk you through the process.

» **Step 1** - Type "San Diego bakery" into the Google search bar and hit enter. http://www.twiggs.org/ came up top in the search results.

» **Step 2** – Go to SEMRush.com and run a report on their overall Google compliance score. Their overall score right now is a 78% out of a possible 100%, which is like getting a letter grade of a C.

» **Step 3** – Go to https://www.google.com/webmasters/tools/mobile-friendly/ and run a report on their overall Google mobile compliance score. Unfortunately, Google is showing their website is not mobile friendly.

» **Step 4** – Go to http://freetools.webmasterworld.com/ and click on "Indexed Pages" to determine how many pages of content the Twiggs.org people have. Currently, they have 176 pages of content on their website (each page must have 1,000 words or more).

» **Step 5** – Go to SEMRush.com again to check how many backlinks the good people at www.Twiggs.org have. Currently they have 4,100 backlinks.

Equipped with this information, you now know that if you wanted to beat Twiggs.org for the term "San Diego bakery," you would need to have the following:

» Google architecture compliance score of 79% or more.

» A Google mobile compliance score that is found to be "mobile friendly."

» 352 pages of original content on your website (because you always want to have two times more content that your closest competition).

» 8,000 backlinks from various websites around the internet.

» Thus, your total costs needed to win would be approximately:

    » $3,000 to fix your website to get it both architecturally and mobile compliant.

>» $3,520 to pay for the writing of 352 pages of original content for you.

>» $16,000 to create 8,000 backlinks from various high quality websites around the internet.

In total, you would need to invest approximately $22,520 to win.

Quick Thoughts from Clay:

Marinate on the math for a moment. For me, this number would be very encouraging both now and when I was starting my first business out of my college dorm room. I grew up without money. When I was in college, I worked at a call center, Applebee's, Target and as an intern at Tax and Accounting Software Company. I worked nearly 80 hours per week during the summer as a home health aide at night and a very low-skilled construction worker during the day. Without reservation, I spent nearly $2,000 per month on Yellow Page advertisements and nearly $1,000 per month on bridal fairs – this while I was still in college. To afford this marketing, both my wife and I decided to live without air conditioning and to operate with one mobile phone and one car. We made sacrifices, but they paid off. If I owned a bakery in San Diego and I just discovered that for a total outlay of $22,520 I could beat my competition, I would be pumped and asking when we could get started!

Once you have determined your winnable keywords, it is time to begin the process of executing the proven winning strategy, which includes the following steps, that we will teach you in a minute:

>» **Step 1** – Create a website with the proper Google compliant website architecture

>» **Step 2** – Create a website that is Google mobile compliant

>» **Step 3** – Set up Google Places

>» **Step 4** - Gather Reviews

>» **Step 5** - Create the most relevant and keyword-rich original content possible

>» **Step 6** - Generate the most high-quality backlinks

The SEO Manifesto:

Search engine optimization is about getting in front of your ideal and likely buyers who are already searching for the solutions your company provides. If you are not on page one of Google's search engine results, you are invisible to customers...which is only cool if you are trying to hide from additional revenue, customers, and money.

Who Is Truly in Charge of Google Search Engine Results?

Google earns their money by creating the best search engine results possible for people who search the internet. If no one is using their search engine because the results that they are displaying are not logical and relevant, soon Google will not be able to make any money from selling advertising. Thus, they are obsessed with making their search engine results the best in the world. As it relates to search engines, Google is the boss, the referee, the judge, and always the final word on who is deemed the "most relevant" website. If you follow their rules, you win. If you choose to not follow their rules for artistic, personal or psychological reasons, you will lose.

When in doubt, refer to Wikipedia. Google loves Wikipedia in the way that Thrive15.com's founder will always love Tom Brady and the Patriots. Google loves Wikipedia because Wikipedia has chosen to follow all of the rules of search engine optimization on a mass scale.

Why Is Google Always Changing?

Google is focused on providing the most relevant search engine results possible, so they can convince more people to use their search engine when they are looking for the products and services they both want and need. The more people who are using Google, the more money they can charge advertisers. As technology has evolved, Google has had to evolve as well. As Google evolves, your business must also evolve if you want your customers to continue to be able to find you when searching the internet.

The Magic Begins on Mobile

We must design our websites to look great on mobile devices because this is what the majority of internet users (90%) are using to view our websites. We must also design our websites to look and work great on mobile devices because Google now requires websites to meet its mobile compliance standards if they are going to rank highly in search engine results. To see how highly or lowly Google is ranking your website, just shoot us an e-mail at info@ThriveTimeShow.com and we will run a free report for you.

To make sure you fully understand the necessary components of our search engine optimization system, we will first cover how it works. Then we will teach you how to do it. In order to dominate in Google search engine results, you must take the following action steps.

Step 1 – Create a website with the proper Google compliant website architecture

Your website must follow Google's canonical rules. Your website must follow the Google compliance checklist, which is available at www. ThriveTimeShow.com/TreasureTrove. If you are a normal human, you are probably totally unaware of how your site ranks in terms of its overall architecture and canonical compliance. Don't let this overwhelm you.

Definition Magician:

Canonical Rules - When referring to programming, canonical means conforming to well-established patterns or rules. The term is typically used to describe whether or not a programming interface follows the already established standards. You don't want to build a bizarre website that Google does not understand and thus, won't place high in search engine results.

Step 2 – Create a website that is Google mobile compliant

Your website must meet Google's mobile search compliance rules or you will lose. I realize that you might not like all these rules, but because our good friends at Google are in charge, you'll have to take up any arguments with Larry Page or Sergey Brin (the founders of Google). If you want to check the current mobile compliance of your existing website, visit: https://www.google.com/webmasters/tools/mobile-friendly/.

If the good people at Google ever decide to change this link, please e-mail us at Thrive15.com and we shall help you find the new link. That's what we do.

Step 3 – Set up Google Places

Have you ever used your phone to search for a restaurant when out of town? Have you noticed that the local business listings that pop up at the top of Google search results for certain terms include user reviews and a number of stars appearing near the listing itself? Usually you can see the business' phone number and address there as well. Well that, my friend, is Google Places. OPTIMIZING YOUR GOOGLE PLACES ACCOUNT HAS THE POTENTIAL TO LITERALLY DOUBLE YOUR INCOME. We have worked with countless business owners from nearly every field and industry imaginable (apothecary pharmacies, chiropractors, dentists, fitness companies, lawyers, manufacturers, professional sports teams, and many more) who have been able to literally double the number of inbound calls and leads they were receiving simply by doing this! YOU MUST MAKE THIS HAPPEN. In order to get your company to show up in search engine results and to begin gathering those reviews so that you can show up prominently on Google maps, you will need to fully set up your Google Places account.

Type in "Google My Business" in the Google search field, follow the link and then completely fill out every area of the form in order to have the most robust Google profile. During this step, you will have to provide a real physical address to verify that you are a real business. If you get stuck while attempting to do this, you will not be the first human on the planet who has ever done so. Just e-mail us at info@ThriveTimeShow.com; we will literally pick up the phone, call you and walk you through this process.

While optimizing your Google Places account, make sure you include the following:

1. Confirm that your address is both correct and consistent. If you are operating a home-based business, I recommend that you set up a UPS mailbox and consistently use that address. I realize that this seems blatantly obvious, however, it is CRITICAL that your address remain consistent because of the way Google has set up the local search feature. You need to write your address the exact same way every time, because Google cares about this stuff when ranking websites; therefore, you and I need to care about this stuff. As an example, use either "Ave." or "Avenue" (pick one and stick with it, write it out or abbreviate) every time you set up an online address listing for your company on the internet on websites like YellowPages.com, YEXT, Groupon, Moz, Axciom, InfoGroup, Factual, InsiderPages, Neustar, and the like. Failure to be accurate and consistent will negatively impact your overall ranking in Google. When I teach at workshops and other speaking events, some raise their hands right here and say, "But why does Google make you do that?" I typically respond with, "I don't make Google's rules. My game is to learn them and use them to generate copious amounts of money."

2. Verify that your hours of business are accurate. Many people now use Google to search for everything and they blindly trust Google to be right about everything. Think about how much money you could be losing if your Google listing says that you are closed during hours when, in fact, you are open. Unfortunately, most businesses discover that their hours are listed incorrectly when they go through this checklist.

3. Verify that your business is listed in the correct category. For most business owners like you, choosing the category that you are in is not confusing. As an example, if you serve food and you are a restaurant, you would obviously choose to be listed in the "restaurant" category. However, for industries such as public relations, marketing and advertising, you may need to put some thought into the matter to determine which category will generate the most calls to your business. You don't want to be oddly missing from Google search results in a business category that you should be dominating. Unfortunately, when diligent people like you take the time to audit their Google My Business listing, they often find that their business categories are incorrectly set up. Recently, we worked with a mortgage broker whose business was incorrectly listed under the restaurant category. You can imagine that this had a devastating impact on the number of inbound calls he was receiving.

4. Add at least three to five paragraphs of really good content about your business. In this description, make sure to include the name of the local city you are in and how your company can uniquely solve the problems of your ideal and likely buyers.

5. Add as many high-quality photos of your business, your checkout area, your offices and your products and services as Google will allow. Photos really do make a huge impact. In fact, the majority of internet users today tend to gravitate towards websites that are filled with beautiful images and video. At the time of this writing, we are managing the online marketing campaigns for hundreds of business owners just like you. These business owners are always blown away when we show them their weekly website traffic analysis and they see for themselves how their website's visitors explore their website. Well over 80% of the people who visit a website do so using their mobile phone, and they tend to scroll up and down the website rapidly, stopping mainly on compelling photos, videos and a phone number to call. Most business owners fail on this step because they upload poor quality photos to their Google My Business listing. Doing this gives the impression that you are either a hillbilly or the owner of a poorly run business. People shouldn't judge us, but they do.

6. Consider adding a 360-degree view or a virtual tour of your business. If you've ever used Google maps, you are undoubtedly familiar with the feature known as "street view." When you click this view, you can walk around the street and actually get a 360° view of a neighborhood, street, or area. Although this is as disturbing as it is great, many consumers prefer to take a 360° virtual tour of your business before deciding whether or not to engage with your business. Again, if you are going to add this feature, you want to do it right.

7. Write a solid, engaging, and complete introduction to your business. This is the section where you describe your actual business. During this section of your listing, you should include links and the three carefully selected keywords you are focused on optimizing. For instance, if you are a Tulsa-based orthodontist, you would want to focus on including the keyword phrases "Tulsa Orthodontist, Orthodontists Tulsa, Orthodontists in Tulsa."

8. Include the types of payment that you accept. You must be thorough when filling out your Google My Business account, even if it seems to be a waste of time. Believe me, it is not. If two businesses are equally matched, the Google My Business listing that is the most complete and most optimized will win.

Step 4 – Gather Reviews

Google has decided to put the most optimized registered local business with the most "authentic" positive reviews at or near the top of Google search engine results. This means that not only must you properly optimize your local Google business listing, but you and I must also start being very proactive about getting some reviews. You cannot afford to sit back and wait for Google reviews to come to you. Go get those reviews. Unlike our good friends at Yelp, who actually penalize business owners for asking for reviews (don't get me started), our buddies at Google allow you and me to ask our customers for reviews. This is great because once you have the most complete Google My Business account and the most reviews in your area, you will climb to the top of Google search results quickly, even if the reviews you have are not good.

Most business owners fail here by passively waiting for their customers to provide them with reviews and acting as though the negative reviews that have been written don't impact the buying decisions of potential customers. In this world of anonymous reviews, the trolls can quickly gain control, so you must proactively e-mail, call, and ask your happy customers to write a review for you. Most sane people will not typically go out of their way to request reviews.

If you are not proactive about asking for reviews from your happy customers, you will wake up one morning and discover that you have four negative reviews and no positive reviews. After working with thousands of businesses all over the planet, we have developed a pre-written e-mail that has proven to be very effective at helping good business owners like you generate positive reviews. However, I want to add this quick note. In nearly every market on the planet, we find that local business owners have to deal with disgruntled ex-employees, ex-spouses, competitors, and irate customers who are wrong. My friend, you must embrace the truth that this group of humans will be the only people writing reviews about your business if you are not intentional about gathering positive Google reviews.

You must respond to the reviews you have, particularly the negative reviews. I realize that you are not an idiot and that you weren't born yesterday, but I want to make sure that you fully understand this concept. If handled correctly, a negative review can actually provide you with an opportunity to improve the quality of your business and earn the loyalty of both current and potential customers who are watching to see how you will respond. If you come across as an irate business owner and personally attack everyone who gives you anything less than a five-star review, this is not good. Most business owners screw up this step by responding poorly to negative reviews. Respond sincerely and kindly and you will come out ahead.

To bring some clarity to what we just talked about, I have included a screenshot of a typical Google search listing on the following page.

Invest the time to call, text, and email every customer and human you know who has anything favorable to say about your business and ask them to write a review. Choosing not to do this is committing Google suicide, which, unfortunately, I have watched many business owners do over the years. Google has stated repeatedly that you are not allowed to pay people to write favorable reviews, so don't offer money for reviews. For the sake of repetition, just call, text, and email every customer and human you know who has anything positive to say about your business and ask them for a review. We will gladly share our proven, effective template email, text, and call script if you request them by e-mailing info@ThriveTimeShow.com.

Deep Thoughts from the Devil's Advocate:

Q: What if I don't want to ask people to write reviews and I just want them to come about organically?

A: You will be poor.

. . . .

Step 5 – Create the most relevant and keyword-rich original content possible

Perhaps you've been online searching the phrase "free range chickens" or the word "dog" or the name "Ryan Tedder" and you noticed Wikipedia's page at or near the top of nearly every internet search you perform. Perhaps you think it's odd that I would use the phrase "free range chickens" as an example... but we move on.... Have you ever asked yourself why our good friends at Wikipedia are nearly always near the top of Google search results? My friend, it's because Wikipedia follows nearly every one of Google's search engine compliance rules and they have more HTML text content than anyone else about that given subject.

Definition Magician:

(HTML) Hypertext Markup Language - A standardized system for tagging text files to achieve font, color, graphic, and hyperlink effects on World Wide Web pages. This markup is what tells the internet browser how to show website images and words to the user.

So how do you generate more content than nearly anyone else about a given subject? You must write your content following these six steps if you ever plan to get to the top of Google search results during your living years (after we are dead, I'm not sure that you or I care if we are at the top in Google search results anymore).

Step A – Buy the Nuance Dragon Headset, which allows you to turn your talk into text. Basically, this device transcribes the words you speak into pages of text. Remember, you must have more original and keyword rich text on your website than your competition. This headset makes generating that content a little bit easier since you can just talk and the headset and your computer do the rest of the work. Buy this device on Amazon or at http://www.nuance.com.

Step B – Commit to writing more content than any of your competitors about the search term results that you are focused on winning. When you are writing this content, make sure that you reference the keyword that you are focused on winning, such as "Tulsa orthodontists," at least six times per 1,000 words. Here is where the headset mentioned in Step 1 comes into play. Typically, 10 minutes of speaking will produce approximately 1,000 words of original relevant content. Google wants every page of your website to contain at least 1,000 words of content. Why, you ask? We are not to question why. Google is the boss and that is what they want, so that is what we shall do. In order to actually generate this content, you must set aside a specific time in your schedule to get this done. In my own core businesses, I pay a team of people to write this type of content for my companies every day. Yes, I said every day. You must have more original, relevant, and keyword-rich content than your competition if you want to win. To figure out how many pages of original content your competition has, go to http:// freetools.webmasterworld.com.

> "If you cannot do great things, do small things in a great way."
>
> **– *Napoleon Hill***
> **(Bestselling author of** *Think & Grow Rich*)

Step C – Block out a specific time and place every day to write your content. You have to be intentional about this. Don't get nefarious here. Don't look for shortcuts or start copying text from other websites to save time. Google is a multi-billion-dollar company that invests countless dollars annually into catching businesses that are simply copying text from another website. Years ago, a homebuilder reached out to us to help him grow his business and increase the overall effectiveness of his marketing. He asked us to look into why his website was perpetually found at the bottom of Google search results or even not found. After simply using the free tool that is available at http://www.copyscape.com/duplicate-content/, we found our answer. Much to his dismay, we showed him that his website was an exact replica of another website for a business located in the northeast

United States. The web development company he hired to build his website simply copied the text from another homebuilder's website. They apparently assumed he would never check whether his copy was original or not, and they were right. You and I need to be much wiser about how content is created for our websites. Any time that we allow anyone to write content for our websites, we must ensure that it is original. We do this by using the free tool at http://www.copyscape.com/duplicate-content/.

If you ever get the urge to try to save both time and money by reducing the amount of content that you place on each page of your website, please understand that this is not a good idea. Google has a habit of not highly ranking, featuring, or indexing (showing in search results) website pages that do not have at least 1,000 words of content per page.

If you or I are writing our own search engine optimization content, we have to move quickly to create massive amounts of content if we are going to beat our competition. Because of the volume of work involved, you may opt to hire some people to generate content for your business. Determine a pay scale for those people you will employ to write content that will win your chosen search term. As of 2016, I believe that a pay scale that allows your writers to earn around $20-$30 per hour (writing at a rapid pace) is fair. If you disagree, that is fine, but it is important that you

"In the absence of the gold standard, there is no way to protect savings from confiscation through inflation. There is no safe store of value."

- *Alan Greenspan*
(American economist and former chairman of the Federal Reserve)

"Inflation is as violent as a mugger, as frightening as an armed robber, and as deadly as a hit man."

- *Ronald Reagan*
(40th president of the United States)

use a merit-based pay program for your search engine optimization team. Pay your writers what the quality of their content says they are worth. I am not exaggerating when I say that I have literally worked with hundreds and hundreds of business owners who have attempted to pay their search engine optimization content writers either a salary or an hourly wage and in all cases, the quality of the content they generated ranged between horrible and bad.

When evaluating the pay scale you will offer, remember that the geniuses who run both our federal government (Thrivers outside of the United States have problems with their governments too) and state governments don't know how to operate from a balanced budget. Because they generate debt on a weekly and monthly basis, they simply print money when they run out. This printing of money (known as fiat currency) decreases the value of our money each year. This is why the cost of living goes up every year. Keep this in mind and raise the amount you pay your people every two to three years to keep up with inflation.

☺ Fun Fact:

Using the inflation calculator that is available at http://data.bls.gov/, you will quickly discover that a house that costs $238,062.22 in 2016 could have been purchased in 1971 for just $40,000. Thus, Clay Clark and the Thrive15.com team have often thought about investing millions of dollars into the creation of a time machine. Taking money into the past would be great. However, taking money into the future is just scary.

🧙 Definition Magician

"Fiat currency" is legal tender whose value is backed by the government that issued it. The U.S. dollar is fiat money, as are the euro and many other major world currencies. This approach differs from money whose value is underpinned by some physical good such as gold or silver called a commodity.

☺ **Fun Fact:**

In October 1976, the government officially changed the definition of the dollar; references to gold were removed from statutes. From that point on, the international monetary system was made up solely of fiat money. Thus, the government can now spend money on whatever they want without a budget and whenever they run out of money, they can just print more. Good job, government.

•••

Step 6 – Generate the most high-quality backlinks

Link building is the action of acquiring hyperlinks from other websites that link to your own website. Although you cannot control what people do on their websites, you can strongly encourage people to share about your website and add a link from their site to yours. A hyperlink from another website to yours is most often referred to as a "backlink." Google and other search engines will count the number of high quality backlinks that you have pointed toward your website as they crawl around the web in their never-ending quest to determine which site should be awarded the top position in their search engine results.

For those backlinks to be most effective, they must include the proper anchor text. Anchor text basically describes to the search engines the overall subject of the website page that is being linked to. Well-written anchor text will always include the main keywords you are focused on winning. You cannot control the words or actions of the other websites that are linking back to you, but in many cases, the individuals running those sites will ask you for a suggestion of what text you would like to be displayed in the backlink. Let me give you an example:

Score Basketball is proud to provide the best Tulsa basketball lessons in the region. For over 30 years, Coach Calvert and his team have provided northeast Oklahoma's most well-known and results-focused Tulsa basketball camps and personal Tulsa basketball coaching experience.

In this example, "Tulsa basketball lessons" serves as the anchor text. Those are the keywords this business owner is focused on winning. When Google sees that you and I have received a high-quality backlink from a website that is using text like this, it celebrates this activity by moving us higher and higher up those Google search results.

Although you could spend a nuclear half-life in the internet researching the various theories of search engine optimizers, bloggers and academics, I am going to make your life easier by listing for you here the EIGHT SUPER MOVES that work.

1. Creating Link Magnets

2. Create Link Bait

3. Gather Online Citations for Your Business

4. Guest Blogging and Podcasting

5. Guest Article Writing

6. Testimonial Links

7. Blog Writing (on your own website)

8. Asking Your Business Network to Link to You

1. Link Magnets

When I mention link magnets, I am referring to the various elements of your website that have been created in such a way that humans with a functional brain will naturally want to link to them. In the same way that certain magnets attract certain metals, these quick moves that I am going to teach you will attract backlinks to your website as people find it to be both valuable and engaging. This process takes time to fully establish itself, but I have seen it work for many businesses, including my own.

As an example, the resources that we make available at www. ThriveTimeShow.com/TreasureTrove are useful and are often linked to by business owners who benefited from using them.

2. Link Bait

When we refer to link bait, we are referencing a steroid-enhanced version of a link magnet. Basically, link bait is something on your website that is intentionally designed to appeal to emotions or be engaging or provocative to get another human to provide a backlink to your site. A tremendous example of link bait is The Dollar Shave homepage (https://www.dollarshaveclub.com/). The video that is located on this home page has been viewed millions of times and is often linked to by other people who sincerely enjoy the commercial and just want to share it with others. Years ago, the world began to hear about Blendtec blenders because of their hilarious videos found on Blendtec's Youtube channel. Go check them out and you will quickly see why millions of people willingly provided a link to both the Blendtec videos and their website. They are hilarious and they showcase the product's actual blending power.

3. Gather Online Citations for Your Business

A citation is when another website references your business name, phone number, and address as listed on your website. The most common citations come from places you are probably familiar with: BingPlaces.com, Google.com/business, InsiderPages.com, SuperPages.com, Yelp.com, FourSquare.com, MerchantCircle.com, 411.com, Mapquest.com, and other sites like that. You see, our good friends at Google use citations to help them decide whether or not your business should be considered a relevant entity in their Knowledge Graph. The Google Knowledge Graph is an incredibly large base of knowledge that is used by Google in its never-ending pursuit to improve its already massive search engine results. Google's "disturbingly large" semantic search data is being continuously gathered from a variety of sources. As you talk or type into your phone the various items that you are using Google to look for, Google is learning more and more about you so that it can accurately (some say "disturbingly accurately") begin to understand your intent and predict what the most relevant search results should be just for you. The semantic search project is yet another massive project Google has taken on to dramatically enhance the consistency and accuracy of the search results generated for its users. The best tools to speed along the creation of hundreds of high-quality citations for your website are Yext.com and Moz.com/Local. These are both paid services that we use when working with our clients and in our own business ventures.

4. Guest Blogging and Podcasting

If you are an expert in your field and are willing to commit the time needed to produce accurate, insightful and helpful content that can be either listened to or read by your ideal and likely buyers, then you should reach out to the various bloggers and podcasters within your niche to see if you can be a guest contributor for their blog or podcast. When you produce a quality piece of content, most bloggers and podcasters will provide a link back to your website from their website, thus generating a high-quality and relevant backlink from a trusted source within your industry. For additional trainings on the specifics of how to systematically reach out to the top podcasters and bloggers within your niche, visit www.ThriveTimeShow.com/TreasureTrove.

5. Guest Article Writing

If you love to write or at least have the ability to generate expert and compelling content that your ideal and likely buyers are willing, and maybe even want to read, you should reach out to various online publications to become a guest writer / contributor. Forbes.com, FastCompany.com and Entrepreneur.com are all top-rated sites that feature content on a consistent basis produced by guest writers.

6. Testimonial Links

If you have provided an extremely high level of satisfaction to your ideal and likely buyers, you need to begin gathering testimonial links from your clients. Basically, a testimonial link is a backlink to your website that is found within a paragraph that contains a large amount of sincere, relevant information touting your website as a source of wisdom and knowledge.

Your customers' websites may contain a page dedicated to explaining how they are proud to partner with great vendors like you. Consider this example:

In Tulsa you can find a large variety of restaurants and bakeries that serve gourmet cookies. However, for the best cookies in Tulsa, you need to experience Barbee's Tulsa cookies. Barbee's has delicious cookies of all shapes and sizes and you can even now buy her cookies online. When we need to send our clients a special gift, without reservation, we use BarbeeCookies.com and you should too.

7. Blog Writing (on your own website)

If you invest both the time and effort to create quality blogs and articles on your website that actually provide useful or entertaining information, many people will naturally want to link back to your website. When you write an article that is non-sales oriented, educational, informative, or entertaining, people will begin to link to you quite often. To make your life 2% better, I have provided a few examples of what I am talking about.

» Articles about topical and hot news issues: Writings about Justin Bieber's most recent attempt to get in trouble, Donald Trump saying something polarizing, or Great Britain's decision to leave the European Union as part of the Brexit movement are all examples of this kind of article. Perez Hilton has made a great living writing these kinds of articles: http://perezhilton.com/category/justin-bieber/ - .V4uLs5MrLMI

» Humorous or engaging content: If you are Jedi Master when it comes to writing funny stories about topics that humans enjoy, then this may just be your super move for generating high-quality backlinks. If you recorded a daily video blog or a weekly podcast or wrote a daily blog about your unique perspective on life, your fans will begin to want to share your content with their friends. As they begin to share, more and more high-quality backlinks will pour in. As an example, the good people at WestJet Airlines invested the time, money and energy into creating a video that has been shared by some 45 million to date. You can check out the video at https://www.youtube.com/watch?v=zIEIvi2MuEk.

» How-to guides: When you take the time needed to thoroughly explain how to do something in both an easy and concise way using visuals, videos, text, or infographics, people will naturally begin to share backlinks to your website. The Pioneer Woman (Ree Drummond) is a powerful example of somebody who is now making millions of dollars and generating thousands of backlinks thanks to her powerful How-to Guides. Visit her website at http://thepioneerwoman.com/cooking/.

» Top Ten lists: David Letterman feasted on the power of Top Ten lists during his career as a late night talk show host, and you can too. When you write a helpful top ten list related to your industry, people will share it time and time again. Some examples of this are the Top Ten Ways to Be a Better Dad, the Top 10 Ways to Save More Money, and the Top Ten Ways to Properly Feed and Raise Organic Free Range Chickens. People will provide the backlinks you need if they find your content to be helpful. As an example, the powerful entrepreneurial podcast, Entrepreneurs On Fire, published a blog post titled, "Top 15 Business Books Recommended by Today's Top Entrepreneurs." That list has been shared 589 times, as of the writing of this book. See this blog post by going to http://www.eofire.com/top-15-business-books-recommended-todays-top-entrepreneurs/.

» Resources: If you and your team (which might consist of you and yourself) are willing to invest the time to document new research, surveys, case studies, compelling charts, infographics, or interesting graphs, this will also create backlinks to your website over time. We've employed this tactic ourselves as over the years, we have added dozens and dozens of practical resources, templates, and downloadables for entrepreneurs and business owners like you. These have generated plenty of backlinks for our site. Check out what we've done by visiting www.ThriveTimeShow.com/TreasureTrove.

8. Asking Your Business Network to Link to You

Many business relationships are very symbiotic, meaning that both parties need each other to be successful. To give you an idea of how this can work, years ago we helped a general family doctor generate nearly 100 high-quality backlinks by convincing suppliers, the insurance reps, the pharmaceutical sales reps, and other people with whom he did business to provide a link on their website to his using the proper anchor text. Why did they do this?

They did this because the good doctor agreed to feature them in his on-going podcast, and because as his practice grew, many of these vendors benefited as a direct result of his success. The more patients he sees, the more supplies he orders and the more prescriptions he writes, and the list goes on and on.

Bonus Step – Get it done.

I think Walt did a great job explaining this bonus step succinctly. Now that you and I know what to do, it really is up to us to just get it done. You

> "One great way to get started is to quit talking and start doing."
> — *Clay Clark*

must schedule both the time and the location you need to get your daily search engine optimization done and done. If you are struggling with your time management skills, we highly recommend that you check out the time management training segment on Thrive15.com, developed by the former Executive Vice President of Walt Disney Resorts, Lee Cockerell, who once managed over 40,000 team members.

Now that we have covered the concepts involved in optimizing a website, it is now time to get into the nuts and bolts, the nitty-gritty step-by-step checklist involved in properly executing an on-going search engine optimization strategy. If you were looking for light reading or even fun reading, this chapter is not it, but I'll do my best.

The Nuts and Bolts of Search Engine Optimization:

> "With self-discipline, almost anything can be achieved in every aspect of life. Those without self-discipline will end up as a poor sloth by default."
> – *Clay Clark*

1. Understanding the Equation (You must know this, so we repeat it often)

2. The mechanics of optimizing website content

3. Uploading Articles / Text Content Checklist

4. Fixing SEMRush Report Errors

The Google Domination Equation

Proper Google Website Architecture (must follow Google's canonical rules) + Proper Google Mobile Compliance + Reviews + Most Relevant Original Content + Most High Quality Backlinks = Top of Google Search Engine Results.

Note: *The managers and business owners who actually care about what they are doing and who are diligent about what they are doing, will win.*

Note: *When building and optimizing a website, you must use a WordPress based website and the Yoast SEO plugin. If you decide to build a custom website instead of using a WordPress-based website with the Yoast SEO plugin, you are going to struggle endlessly with countless issues. The action items below have been written assuming that you are using a WordPress based website and the Yoast SEO plugin.*

Every time you choose to add content to your website, you must optimize each and every page of your website. Listed below is a checklist of all of the steps that you must do correctly on each and every website page.

Optimizing Website Content

1. _____H1 Tag Prioritize (H1 stands for header 1)

   a. You must include the keyword within the first sentence of the content.

   b. This text must be in complete sentence form.

   c. DO NOT EVER DUPLICATE H1 text on other pages of your website. Google hates this and thus, I HATE IT TOO.

   d. Example of well written H1 Tag – *Are you looking for the best haircuts in Tulsa?*

   Step 1: Select the Page or Article that you wish to edit

   Step 2: Select text that you want to make H1 text and enlarge it using "Heading 1" in the paragraph field

   Step 3: Make sure that the H1 text is a complete sentence. (ie. Find Tulsa Men's Haircuts at the Elephant in the Room.)

Step 4: Check again to be sure H1 text is a complete sentence with a subject, verb and a period.

Step 5: Be sure the H1 text is at the top of the page.

2. _____ Article Description (This isn't the meta description)

 a. Make sure to include a title for all content that you are writing, just like you would if you were writing a college paper.

 b. Below the actual title of the content on each page, you must write the description.

 c. DO NOT EVER DUPLICATE the description text or any text.

 d. The phone number should appear on the top of every web page where content is being written.

 » Example - *This article is about how to find a quality men's haircut in Tulsa.*

 » Example - *This business coaching blog is about how to create a pro-forma that is usable.*

3. _____ Keywords (This isn't the meta keywords)

 a. Use the keyword that you are focusing on six times per 1000 words.

 b. The keyword you are focusing on must actually be woven into the article or blog content.

 » Example / Sample Paragraph: *At Elephant in the Room Men's Grooming Lounge, we are focused on providing the very best Owasso haircut. In fact, since first opening our doors at 1609 South Boston in the heart of downtown Tulsa, we have been able to grow our business exponentially as a result of focusing relentlessly on providing a premium grooming experience every time. Now as we expand out just to the north of Tulsa, we are excited about bringing the very best Owasso haircut to this rapidly growing city.*

4. _____ Content / Text

 a. A minimum of 1,000 words of original high-quality content must be created per page of the website you are focused on optimizing.

 b. Producing 1,000 words of content is equal to spending approximately 10 minutes talking on a talk-to-text Dragon headset.

c. I would highly discourage you from attempting to write the content needed for your website's optimization by typing. I would strongly encourage you to use a talk-to-text transcription technology like Dragon so that you can save your time, money and sanity.

d. When creating content, make sure to answer the following questions as you talk into the Dragon headset.

> » Who is this content being written for?
> » Who is ideally searching for this content?
> » What is this content about?
> » Why does this content matter?
> » What do you want your reader to do as a result of this content?
> » Why are you passionate about this content?
> » How is your company different from everybody else in the market?

e. As you create content, you want to make sure that it will be scored highly by Google. In order to score highly, you must include synonyms related to the topic that you are focused on optimizing and you must receive a high readability score.

f. Content that receives a high READABILITY SCORE from Google will rank higher. Readability scores will be higher if you actually make sense and are saying something of meaning. Include synonyms and other industry related terms in your content. I highly encourage you to do a Wikipedia search for the keywords that you are focused on optimizing, then write down six words and terms related to the keyword. Focus on weaving these terms into each article that you write.

> » Example - *http://eitrlounge.com/articles/tulsa-barbershops-elephant-in-the-room-mens-grooming-lounge-best-south-tulsa-barbershop/.*

g. Use proper punctuation. Avoid long run-on sentences. Spell things correctly. Check your work after the article is written.

h. Company names, awards and personal names must be capitalized (Command 'Caps On')

i. The content of the article must be relevant to the company and always truthful.

j. All articles must be written in "Text Edit" and saved as an .RTF (no Word documents allowed). If you choose to save every file as a Word Document (.docx), you will pay for it later as you are forced to reformat all the content that you add to the website. When you save a file as a Word document, it makes the process of uploading the content 30% harder.

k. You must verify whether content has been copied from another website by using http://www.copyscape.com/duplicate-content/.

5. _____ Upload to Dropbox.com (You must keep it organized)

a. You cannot allow your files to become disorganized by default. You must hold your team accountable for keeping your files organized.

b. Upload content to SEO Master Folder / Company Folder

c. Upload content to the correct Writer Folder using the initials of the writer first, the keyword that you / they are focused on second, and the article number third.

d. Create Keyword Folder for articles

 » Example: *CMH – Haircuts in Tulsa*

 » Example: *CMH – Haircuts in Tulsa – 1, CMH – Haircuts in Tulsa – 2, etc...*

6. _____ Fill Out Article Sheet (Insist that all content that is produced is turned in to your company's SEO Manager)

a. A third party must verify the quality of all content.

b. Run a test on all content via CopyScape.com to verify that content has not been plagiarized.

7. _____ Create More Relevant Content than Anyone in Your Niche

Step 1: Determine how much content your competition has had indexed by Google using this incredible tool: http://freetools.webmasterworld.com/. Click on "Indexed Pages."

Step 2: YOU CANNOT EVER DUPLICATE CONTENT. Doing this is like inviting Satan into your website. Google will flag your website for duplicate content and your website will drop like a rock from search engine results. Check for duplicate content using: http://www.copyscape.com/duplicate-content/

Step 3: Don't stop writing until you have written more high-quality and original text than your competition. Search around your office for original content that you have written in the past and get that uploaded to your website. Many companies have a gold mine of thousands of pages of transcripts or original content sitting on a computer somewhere. Use it.

8. _____ Featured Image (Add a new image for each article)

a. Every image that you add to your website must be optimized.

b. You must own the rights to every image that you add to your website.

c. At Thrive15.com, we subscribe to GettyImages.com and IStockPhoto.com so that we can use the massive library of high-quality images both of these companies have carefully organized, paid for and archived.

Step 1: Select a place to put the image.

Step 2: Click on Add Media.

Step 3: Click on Upload Image (must be an image that you have the rights to).

Step 4: Name the image.

  » When you save the image, use dashes. Example: owasso-mens-haircuts.

  » When you title the image, use the same words, but remove the dashes.

Step 5: Set the image to medium size.

Step 6: Set the image to the left side of the page.

Step 7: Use the formatting buttons to wrap the text around the image.

Step 8: Title the image following this format:

  » Example: Owasso Men's Haircut | Shaving Tools

  » Example: Business Coaching | Woman in a Coffee Shop

Step 9: Name the Alt text: same as the title image.

  » No description of image is needed.

Uploading Articles / Text Content Checklist

Once you are ready to upload the content that you and your team have written for your website, it is very important that you follow this checklist. Keep a log of uploaded content that includes the following details:

» Article Uploaded #: _____

» Initials of Uploader:_____

» Date of Article Upload: _____

» Keyword: _____

1. _____ Add Content to Website: No duplicate content is allowed.

   a. Go to Dropbox > SEO Master Folder > Articles

   b. Find the Client (Your Company's) Folder > Choose Writer Folder > Choose Keyword Folder

2. _____ Login to Client Website > Choose Posts / Articles

3. _____ Copy and Paste TWO 500 Word Articles into the Body (or one 1,000 word article)

4. _____ Scroll Down to the Yoast SEO Plugin

5. _____ Meta Title (Referred to as the "Snippet Editor" in SEO Yoast)

   a. Must not include more than nine words (less than 56 characters)

   b. Must include a "vertical bar" = | (located above the return / enter key)

   c. Must include the keyword and article title

      » Example – *Men's Haircuts in Tulsa | (Article Title)*

      » Example - *Men's Haircuts in Tulsa | Find a Superior Cut*

6. _____ Meta Description

   a. Write content that you want to show up on the actual Google search results.

   b. Keep this to two sentences, maximum. Include the keyword in the first sentence.

   c. Include the phone number / call to action in the second sentence.

    d.   This content must fit into the SEO Yoast character rule limit.

       » Example: *Are you looking for a premium south Tulsa Men's haircut? Call the award-winning Elephant in the Room team at 918-877-2219.*

       » Example: *In this article, award-winning business coach teaches management with the former EVP of Disney World, Lee Cockerell. Sign up for a free trial today.*

7. _____ Add the One "Focus Keyword"

    a.   SEO Yoast will ask you to determine one "Focus Keyword" that you are focused on.

    b.   Choose the "Focus Keyword" for SEO Yoast based upon what keyword phrase the content you are uploading was focused on.

    c.   Provide six tag phrases (keyword phrases) that pertain to the keyword you are focusing on that can be found within the content that you are uploading.

    d.   The keywords that you list must be included in the actual article.

       » Example - *Business Coaching*

       » Example – *How to grow a business, business coach, coaching businesses, how to find a business coach, business coach, accounting*

8. _____ Add Optimized Permalink (Also known as a "Slug" in SEO Yoast)

    a.   The focused keyword that you are currently uploading content for must be included in the permalink.

    b.   Do not attempt to automate this process. When you create an automated process, you will start to create duplicate content and Google will penalize you.

    c.   Every permalink must be different.

       » Example - *http://www.eitrlounge.com/find-tulsa-mens-haircuts*

9. _____ Compose Anchor Text Found Within Content

    a.   You must include your keyword six times within every 1,000 words of your article and you must provide a link from this phrase out to content that relates to it (within your own website, if possible).

b.   Wikipedia uses anchor text everywhere. For an example of how they do it, go to https://en.wikipedia.org/wiki/Dog. Wikipedia has a hyperlink (a link to another webpage) embedded for the word "Canidae," "domesticated canid," "selectively bred," "Eurasia," and other words and phrases. When you click each of the phrases, you are taken to another section of Wikipedia's massive library of content. This is what you want on your website. Granted, you may not be as massive as Wikipedia, but you at least want to provide a few links out to related content found within your website. As an example, if you had content that mentioned the city of Orlando, you would either want to provide a link to a portion of your website that discusses the city of Orlando or you would want to provide a link out to the City of Orlando's website (http://www.cityoforlando.net/).

c.   Hyperlink out from words related to your OPTIMIZATION FOCUS to sites of high quality and integrity (high page rank).

» Example - *At the Elephant in the Room, we guarantee that you will love your Tulsa men's haircut (link this text to our website).*

10.   _____ Embed a Video

a.   Pages featuring YouTube videos are ranked higher in Google search engine results.

b.   Remember, Google owns YouTube. If you were Google, wouldn't you rank websites higher that include content found within YouTube than websites that include content found within Vimeo?

c.   Adding videos to your web pages also increases the time that each visitor spends on each webpage, which increases your score. Google sincerely cares about the user experience and they want to reward websites that are able to keep people engaged and on a website longer.

d.   The video should be embedded right below the text written for it.

Step 1:   Go to YouTube to find a video

Step 2:   On Youtube.com, find a video THAT WAS CREATED BY YOUR COMPANY or by the client that you are optimizing for. You MUST select a video from the client's YouTube channel.

Step 3:   On YouTube.com, click the Share button

Step 4:   On YouTube.com, click the Embed button

Step 5:   On YouTube.com, copy code into Article / Update

Step 6:   On the WordPress-based website, switch from Visual to Text

Step 7:   On YouTube.com, select video size: 640 x 360

Step 8:   On YouTube.com, uncheck the box that says "Show suggested videos"

Step 9:   On YouTube.com, copy the iframe embed code

Step 10:   On the WordPress-based website, go back to your article

Step 11:   Paste the iFrame embed code into the article right below the text written for it. (ie: This content is written for *client name*)

Step 12:   On the WordPress-based website, switch back to the Visual tab to verify the video is actually there

Step 13:   On the WordPress-based website, click Update

Step 14:   On the WordPress-based website, open "View Article" in a new window to preview your work

Step 15:   On the WordPress-based website, press Play to verify the embedded video works

Step 16:   On the WordPress-based website, verify that no related videos pop up at the end of the embedded video

11. _____ Name All Images Correctly

a. Make sure to name all images based upon your search engine strategy.

   » Example - On EITRLounge.com, the images appearing on that page should be labeled "*tulsa-mens-haircut-example-1*," and "*tulsa-mens-haircut-example-2*."

Step 1:   Select a place to put the image.

Step 2:   Click on Add Media.

Step 3:   Upload the image (must be an original image for each article).

Step 4:   Name the title of the image (when you save the image, use dashes, no spaces - example: *owasso-mens-haircuts*).

Step 5:   When you title the image, use the same words, but remove the dashes.

Step 6:   Set the image to medium size.

Step 7:   Set the image to the left side of the page.

Step 8:   Use the formatting buttons to wrap the text around the image.

Step 9:   Title the image following this format: Owasso Men's Haircut | Shaving Tools Business Coaching | Woman in a Coffee Shop

Step 10:   Name the Alt text: same as the title image.

   » No description of image is needed.

Fixing SEMRush Report related errors

Fixing SEMRush Report related errors

Step 1:   Go to semrush.com

Step 2:   Click log-in and use the appropriate user name and password

Step 3:   Click the + button (located next to Projects)

Step 4:   Choose a name and domain for the project

Step 5:   Click on Site Audit

Step 6:   Crawl all pages and click Start Edit

Step 7:   Click on Site Audit

Step 8:   Click on View All Issues

Step 9:   Once you click View All Issues, a mountain of errors will appear. This checklist tells you how to fix these errors.

1. Alt Tags – Coder must fix.

Step 1:   Use the Divi template found within WordPress. Building a custom website is nearly always a disaster if you do not have full-time coders working for you.

Step 2:   Use the Divi template.

Step 3:   Use the Divi template.

2. Broken Images – A Coder / Web-Development Professional must fix.

3. Doc Type Not Declared – A Coder / Web-Development Professional must fix.

4. Duplicate Description (See the Meta description steps found in section 37.8, point 6.)

5. Duplicate Titles (Someone copied and pasted.)

6. External Links That Are Broken

   Step 1: Click the "external links are broken" link to show all broken URLs

   Step 2: Find 404 Errors to fix. (Ignore all other errors.)

7. HTTPS Encryption – Coder must fix. Google ranks websites higher that have invested the time and energy needed to install a Secure Socket Layer (SSL) as a sublayer under regular HTTP application layering. Whenever you use HTTPS on your website, you are choosing to make your website more secure, and Google loves this.

8. Internal Links that Are Broken – A Coder / Web-Development Professional must fix.

9. Low Text to HTML Ratio – A Coder / Web-Development Professional must fix.

10. Missing H1 Heading – To create a proper H1 heading, review the trainings found in the previous two sections of this book.

11. Missing Robots.txt

    Step 1: Click Plugins in the left sidebar

    Step 2: Click the Add New button at the top

    Step 3: In the Search Plugins bar, search for: Yoast SEO

    Step 4: Click Install Now button

    Step 5: Click the blue Activate link

    Step 6: Go to SEO Tools Tab

    Step 7: Click on File Editor

    Step 8: Click Robot.txt button (this button tells Google which pages it can crawl)

12. More than H1 Heading – A Coder / Web-Development Professional must fix.

13. No Follow Attributes – A Coder / Web-Development Professional must fix.

14. Page that Returns 4XX Status Code

   Step 1:   Locate the broken link

   Step 2:   Delete the link OR link it to something that does exist

15. Pages that Cannot Be Crawled - Coder must fix.

16. HTML Sitemap (HTML = Humans to See… It MUST be visible! MUST be referred to as "sitemap" at the bottom of the page.)

   Step 1:   Go to Pages

   Step 2:   Click Add New button at the top

   Step 3:   Title it: Sitemap

   Step 4:   In the right hand column under Page Attributes, select Sitemap from template drop down.

   Step 5:   Click Publish.

17. .XML Sitemap

   Step 1:   Install SEO Yoast

18. HTTPS encryption--Coder must fix.

19. Submit Website to Google Webmaster Tools

   Step 1:   Must set up a Gmail account

   Step 2:   Submit site to Yahoo

   Step 3:   Search for Google Search Console

   Step 4:   Login to gmail https://www.google.com/webmasters/tools/home?hl=en

   Step 5:   Add a Property

   Step 6:   Paste the URL of the correct website (ie: https:/eitrlakewood.com)

   Step 7:   Click on Alternate Methods

   Step 8:   Click on HTML Tag

   Step 9:   Copy the metatag below

Step 10:	Login to WordPress website
Step 11:	Go to Appearance in the left bar
Step 12:	Click on Editor
Step 13:	Click Enable Editing
Step 14:	Go to Theme Header on the right
Step 15:	Look for the head within the theme header
Step 16:	Paste the metatag underneath the first head
Step 17:	Click Update File
Step 18:	Click on Verify within the Google Search Console
Step 19:	Click Continue
Step 20:	Verify that you are submitting your website for Google to crawl it within the right country preference
Step 21:	Click Search Traffic
Step 22:	Click on International Targeting
Step 23:	Click on Country and checkmark targeted users in the appropriate country
Step 24:	Click Save
Step 25:	Click on Crawl and Sitemaps
Step 26:	Click Add/Test Sitemap
Step 27:	Enter: sitemap_index.xml
Step 28:	Click Test
Step 29:	Verify there are no errors
Step 30:	Click Close
Step 31:	Click Add/Test Sitemap again
Step 32:	Enter: sitemap_index.xml
Step 33:	Click Submit
Step 34:	Click Refresh - Allow 24 hours for Google to index the site
Step 35:	Click Fetch as Google
Step 36:	Click Fetch and Render
Step 37:	Enter: sitemap_index.xml in the box
Step 38:	Click Fetch and Render again

Step 39: After they're done pending, click Submit to Index for each

Step 40: Select Crawl this URL and its Direct Links

Step 41: Click Go

20. Too Low of a Word Count (must have at least 1000 words on the page)

Step 1: Copy the permalink of the page with not enough content

Step 2: Record the keywords for this page

21. Too Many On-Page Links

Step 1 and Done: If the page is a blog or article, remove any links beyond

Note: Do not remove a heavy amount of links from a "Press Page" that features all of your media wins or from your overall "Sitemap"

22. Too Much Text in the Meta Description--See above

23. Too Much Text in the Meta Title Tag--See above

24. URL Too Long (Slugs and Permalinks)

Step 1 and Done: Follow SEO Yoast guidelines

"ITS HARD TO STEER A PARKED BUS."
— CLAY CLARK

HOP IN GUYS! THIS BUS IS All READY TO GO.

Claymations

The Biblical Ten Commandments
(Found In Exodus Chapter 20: 3-17):

Commandment #1 - [3] Thou shalt have no other gods before me. [4] Thou shalt not make unto thee any graven image, or any likeness of any thing that is in heaven above, or that is in the earth beneath, or that is in the water under the earth. [5] Thou shalt not bow down thyself to them, nor serve them: for I the Lord thy God am a jealous God, visiting the iniquity of the fathers upon the children unto the third and fourth generation of them that hate me; [6] And shewing mercy unto thousands of them that love me, and keep my commandments.

Commandment #2 - [7] Thou shalt not take the name of the Lord thy God in vain; for the Lord will not hold him guiltless that taketh his name in vain.

Commandment #3 - [8] Remember the sabbath day, to keep it holy.

Commandment #4 - [9] Six days shalt thou labour, and do all thy work: [10] But the seventh day is the sabbath of the Lord thy God: in it thou shalt not do any work, thou, nor thy son, nor thy daughter, thy manservant, nor thy maidservant, nor thy cattle, nor thy stranger that is within thy gates: [11] For in six days the Lord made heaven and earth, the sea, and all that in them is, and rested the seventh day: wherefore the Lord blessed the sabbath day, and hallowed it.

Commandment #5 - [12] Honour thy father and thy mother: that thy days may be long upon the land which the Lord thy God giveth thee.

Commandment #6 - [13] Thou shalt not kill.

Commandment #7 - [14] Thou shalt not commit adultery.

Commandment #8 - [15] Thou shalt not steal.

Commandment #9 - [16] Thou shalt not bear false witness against thy neighbour.

Commandment #10 - [17] Thou shalt not covet thy neighbour's house, thou shalt not covet thy neighbour's wife, nor his manservant, nor his maidservant, nor his ox, nor his ass, nor any thing that is thy neighbour's.

The American Bedding Direct 10 Commandments for Achieving Success:

Commandment #1 - Thou shall take responsibility for the success or failure of your business.

Commandment #2 - Thou shall urgently secure a commercial location for your business.

Commandment #3 - Thou shall urgently register a Google Map within your local designated market area.

Commandment #4 - Thou shall gather two times more objective Google reviews than any of the local mattress business competitors within your designated market area.

Commandment #5 - Thou shall diligently meet with your business coach each week to learn what action items you need to take to earn the money you want to make.

Commandment #6 - Thou shall block out the time needed to turn your to-do list into a to-done list.

Commandment #7 - Thou shall gather two times more objective Google reviews than any of the local mattress business competitors within your designated market area.

Commandment #8 - Thou shall measure what you treasure and track where you don't want your business to slack.

Commandment #9 - Thou shall call, text and email your leads until they cry, buy or die.

Commandment #10 - Thou shall gather two times more objective Google reviews than any of the local mattress business competitors within your designated market area.

CHAPTER 5
SCRIPTS
(TALKING IN YOUR SLEEP)

You want your scripts to be so simple, repeatable and effective that they could almost cause you to dream about your scripts and the success they produce for you while you are sleeping.

When creating your scripts, remember the business is really simple and the biggest challenge is keeping it simple. When customers respond to your advertisements for something that you have for sale with enthusiasm and urgency you just allow them to come in and purchase. It's that simple, very similar. If you had a litter of puppies and you had to get rid of every puppy, how would you do it? You'd place an ad, you'd respond to people that inquired about your ad and you schedule a time for them to come look at the puppies. Apply the same method to the mattress business.

Responding to customers by phone or by text message keep the responses short and simple; always be authentic and genuine and excited to clear out your mattress inventory regardless of which mattress the customer is contacting you about.

As a SMART Person You Will Appreciate Our Idiot-Proof Turn-Key Systems & Scripts:

"I try to invest in businesses that are so wonderful that an idiot can run them. Because sooner or later, one will."

WARREN BUFFET

(Warren Edward Buffett is an American investor and philanthropist who is the chairman and former CEO of the conglomerate Berkshire Hathaway. As a result of his success, Buffett is one of the best-known investors in America. According to Forbes, as of January 2026, Buffett's estimated net worth stood at US$148.9 billion, making him the ninth-richest individual in the world.)

When the customers come in to meet you face-to-face at your location again, be consistent with what you told them on the phone or in the messaging. Re-create the sense of urgency and just be yourself, show them what you have and help them get what's best for them. People will buy from you if they like you and trust you and if you have a great product at a great price, what you do just help people find what they're looking for.

Use a script while sounding like you are not reading a script. Be yourself, smile, ask the customer what they're looking for and show them what you have to offer that will meet their needs and solve their problem; give them a reason to buy today. Let them know that you want to clear everything out and then you give them a little bit of a better price if they get it today. Just be yourself, have fun, smile and help people out, that is really the key to success.

Tips on speaking to customers.

1. Smile

2. Be yourself

3. Listen to what the customer wants

4. Find the solution.

"The successful leader must plan his work, and work his plan.
A leader who moves by guesswork, without practical, definite
plans, is comparable to a ship without a rudder. Sooner or later
he will land on the rocks. One of the penalties of leadership
is the necessity of willingness, upon the part of the leader, to
do more than he requires of his followers. Efficient leadership
calls for ability to organize and to master details. No genuine
leader is ever "too busy" to do anything which may be required
of him in his capacity as leader. When a man, whether he is
a leader or follower, admits that he is "too busy" to change
his plans, or to give attention to any emergency, he admits
inefficiency. The successful leader must be the master of all
details connected with his position."

NAPOLEON HILL

*(The best-selling author of Think and Grow Rich. I named my
son Aubrey Napoleon-Hill Clark after Napoleon-Hill because
Napoleon Hill's research, teaching and writing had such a
profound impact on me and my wife.)*

PHONE SCRIPT—The goal is to set up a meeting.

When a customer contacts us, they want to know why the prices are so low, so we need to have an explanation that makes sense. We have created a phone script for you to use that creates a sense of urgency and explains why the prices are so low. The important thing in your phone approach is that you're comfortable and confident in what you're saying. If you believe in what you're saying and how you're saying it, you will be successful. You can tweak it to your own personality so that you can be authentic in your conversation.

When a customer calls us and says, "I just want the mattress that you have advertised," don't let that throw you off. This is a common response that we get all the time. It is just like if you were in a store and a sales person asks, "Can I help you?," and you say, "No, I'm just looking." If someone responds that they just want the mattress that you had advertised, say "That's great! When would you like to come get it?"

I have had so many experiences where people have said over and over again, "All I want is the low-price mattress; I don't want anything else." Later, they come in and end up purchasing something a lot more expensive. The goal of the phone call is to set up a meeting time, NOT to upsell, and NOT to close a sale. The phone call has one purpose only- to set up a meeting.

When I'm responding to customers, whether by phone or text, I'm not trying to sell anything. I'm just trying to make it an easy process for them to come take a look at the mattresses. I often will tell them via phone or text, "Why don't you just come pick one out or we could hold it for you. You can come back and get it when you're ready. ***But they're going quick, so just come and pick one out while they're still available.***"

Always answer a question briefly and then follow up with a question. Do this by voice call or text.

Phone Example

RAPPORT

A. Hey! Thank you for calling _____ Mattress Clearance, this is _____ (your name), how can I help you today?

B. Awesome! I'm always curious, where did you originally hear about us?

   › *Repeat back what they said*

NEEDS

A. Great! Well, I have a bunch of mattresses in all sizes for sale and they're going pretty fast.

B. What size mattress are you looking at buying?

C. I do have _____-sized mattresses in stock right now, I don't have many left and I'm clearing them out this week.

D. I had some space where I could show them to people in _____ (location).

153

BENEFITS

A. I'm not a typical mattress store, I've got a bunch of mattresses for sale marked down significantly over half off retail.

B. I have queen mattresses left for $150, some for $250 and up from there.

C. We also offer financing options for all of our mattresses.

CLOSE

A. What I am doing for people who want to look or pick one out, is I am setting up times to meet and it's 1st come 1st serve from there.

B. When would you like to come look at them?

C. Awesome! Well, I am available _____ (day) at _____ (time). What time is good for you?

D. Great! The address is _____. What's your name?

E. Nice to meet you, (repeat the customers name back). I'll see you _____ (day) at _____ (time).

"Most people are sitting on their own diamond mines. The surest ways to lose your diamond mine are to get bored, become overambitious, or start thinking that the grass is greener on the other side. Find your core focus, stick to it, and devote your time and resources to excelling at it."

GINO WICKMAN

(The legendary business growth consultant, best-selling author and multiple time www.ThrivetimeShow.com Podcast guest.)

Messaging Customers

Respond quickly to customers on phone and facebook marketplace. Using text replacement in your phone makes answering questions quick and easy. The GOAL is to set up a meeting. Keep it simple.

Messaging Examples

PRE-WRITTEN MESSAGE:

Thank you for reaching out! This is Todd, I want you to know that I have received your message and will be reaching out to you shortly!

I look forward to connecting with you! In the meantime, check out what some of my past customers have to say!

Read our reviews - [send link to Google reviews]

Listen to customer testimonials - [send link to testimonials page of website]

INBOUND INQUIRY MESSAGING SCRIPT:

A. Yes! I have a few mattresses still available, everything is marked over half off. I am in Ponte Vedra Beach, close to Nocatee. What I am doing for people that want to look, is setting up times to meet.

> › *Wait for inquiry response*

B. Would you like to come in and take a look at _____(date) at _____(time).

> › *Wait for inquiry response*

C. Great! The address is _____. What's your name? My name is Todd.

> › *Wait for inquiry response.*

D. Nice to meet you _____ (their name). I'll see you _____ (repeat back meeting date and time). I'll be driving a _____ (car color, make and model).

"The difference between great people and everyone else is that great people create their lives actively, while everyone else is created by their lives, passively waiting to see where life takes them next. The difference between the two is living fully and just existing."

MICHAEL GERBER

(The best-selling author of The E-Myth book series, the legendary entrepreneur and multiple-time www. ThrivetimeShow.com podcast guest.)

DEEP THOUGHTS FROM THE MATTRESS KING

" "

The average mattress consumer only shops 1.6 places. So if they're in front of you, if you've got a great product, if you've got a great price, and if they like you, then you're in a great position for them to buy from you.

Darren Conrad

☺ **Fun Fact:**

Americans Do Spend Money On Buying Mattresses - "On average, U.S. residents spent 107 U.S. dollars on mattresses."
https://www.statista.com/topics/4814/mattress-retail-in-the-us/?srsltid=Af mBOord43QPWA_6tksGUUFI_bLBieQGvObrX037RhLbKMbmwX4-vfPi

158

CHAPTER 6

DOOR GREETING & SALES
(REST EASY KNOWING YOU HAVE A PLAN)

Door Greeting and Sales Approach

When the customer meets you at the location to look at the mattresses, we have some tips to make it go as smoothly as possible. First and foremost, you must show validity by showing them the advertised mattress that they originally saw on the ad. This builds trust. Be authentic, listen to customers & help them get what they want. Review the story that you told them on the phone— THIS IS A MUST! Recreate urgency and the need to buy TODAY. Give them a reason to buy NOW!

Mindset

The selling process starts with your mindset. If anyone has ever golfed before, then you know the process. You have to put the ball on the tee, and then you have to prepare to swing. Your mindset is so important at this point. If you're about to tee off, and you think to yourself, "Please don't go in the water; please don't go in the water. I just don't want it to go in the water," that is exactly the wrong mindset. If you are thinking this, when you take your swing, you are definitely going to hit the ball straight in the water! It will go right in the direction that you are thinking about. Your mindset is extremely important- whether that's in sports or in business.

Therefore, when a customer contacts me about a mattress, my mindset is, "I wonder what time they're going to come see me." Since they are the ones who contacted me about buying a mattress, I don't need to try to sell them on buying a mattress. I know they're gong to buy something. It's just a matter of which one they will buy. So, I'm really just an "assistant purchaser" in the sales process. That is the mindset that I use when someone contacts me or when someone comes to meet me to look at mattresses.

Door Greeting

When someone pulls up and starts coming into the location, I want to intentionally and immediately build rapport with that customer. I use the person's name, I look them in the eyes, and I smile. I show them what I have advertised, offering it for sale, and then I share with them that I want to clear out everything quickly. I want to keep the sense of urgency as well as help the customer get what they want. Get everyone on the same page as quickly as you can.

Example

"Hello_____, I am a local business. We had a bunch of mattresses; however, we do not have very many left. They have been going really quick. Just a reminder, I am not a typical store. Everything is new in plastic and marked down over half off. They start over here and are in order by price. (walking down to the advertised mattress set) This is the one for $\rule{2cm}{0.4pt}$, Go ahead and lay on it to see if you like it. I can't go any lower on price for this model, but anything in here I will get you the best price I can. We really just need to clear everything out. It's all first come first serve. So let's find one that works for what you are looking for."

Ask Questions

Make sure to ASK QUESTIONS to find out what the customer wants and then LISTEN to what they say. I usually ask customers, "Do you want something soft? Firm? Inexpensive? What is it you're looking for?" I also will ask questions like, "What do you sleep on now? What don't you like about your mattress?" Is this for you or for a guestroom? Then I share, "You know, most people like this mattress. These are a very popular choice. Everyone loves this one. I've got two of these left." Never lose a sale because of price. Everyone has a price. Drop and drop until you find your customer's price. Remember to sell something to everyone; it's a volume business.

Trying It Out

After the greeting and after recreating that sense of urgency, I walk the customer down the line and show where the mattresses start. I say things like, "This is the queen set for $150; go ahead and lay on it and see how you like it." When you're showing customers the mattresses, it is really important that they lay on them to try them out. If they like it, great. If they don't, then we have other choices. Allowing the customers to lay on the mattress first before they make a purchase is the key to selling a lot of mattresses. Of course, most people don't really like it, or it's not what they're looking for, or they usually say they want something nicer. I tell them to go ahead and lay on it to see how they like it; I tell them it's actually a great value for the price.

Helping Them Choose

I'm just trying to find which mattress is best for the customer. Always make sure to use mattress terminology when talking to people about what they prefer—whether the mattress is firm, soft, etc. Sometimes if you pick one out and suggest it to the customer, it helps them make a decision. Saying things like, "This is the best mattress for you," or saying, "A lot of other people are choosing the same mattress," helps them to be both confident and comforted in their choice. People are truly looking for you to help them make a choice along the way. Other things that you can say are, "I've got two of these left in plastic. How soon can you get it out of here?" or, "Do you know if you can get it delivered yourself, or do you need me to get it delivered to you?" These phrases help keep the conversation moving in a helpful way. I always want to listen to what the customer is looking for and try to solve their problem along the way.

Quoting a Price

When you're quoting a price, always quote the higher price 1st. You can say something like, "Well let's see, this mattress retails for $1,299, but he's letting it go for $550." (Utilize the Clearance center price sheet). You could say, "If you get it today, I could give you a little better deal..." Then BE QUIET!!!!

Haggling Price

My philosophy here is, "I can't go any lower on the price of the one we had advertised; anything else in here I'll give you the best price I can. I'm just trying to clear them all out, so let's just find out what you're looking for." Sometimes I'll even ask people, "Look, if everything here was $150, which one would you choose?" They tell me the one that they would pick, and I say, "Ok, I can't do that one for $150 but you did say that you liked this other one? If I gave you a really good deal on it, would you buy it?" I continue to build rapport, connect with them, and ask questions.

Selling on Deposit

Sometimes customers see a mattress they like, but they don't need it right away. In that case, I tell them, "Most people pick one out, put down a small deposit, and we can hold it for them until they pick it up." If they ask how much the deposit is, I tell them, "Most customers put down 50%. How much would you like to put down?" ***While writing up the order, GET A GOOGLE REVIEW!!***

Common Objections

Remember, the average mattress consumer only shops 1.6 places. So if they're in front of you, if you've got a great product, if you've got a great price, and if they like you, then you're in a great position for them to buy from you. That's why the most important part of this process is to build rapport, to listen, and to guide them into what they actually want.

If the customer objects to the price, I usually say, "Is that too much for you, or too much for the mattress?" Usually, it's too much for them. Then I ask them, "How much would you like to spend?" I take them to the price point $100 higher in the lineup and offer them that mattress set at a discount.

If someone says, "I've seen this mattress at another store for this price," you can respond and say, "Well it's not the same mattress; these are exclusive." Or you could say, "You know what? It is the same mattress; if I gave it to you at that same price, would you buy it for me?"

If somebody says, "Well, I'm going to think about it and come back again," you know that once they leave, they're never coming back. That means my goal is to get them a mattress while they're still there. So I'll ask them, "What is it that you're not sure about? Do you not like the price? Do you not like the feel of the mattress? What is it you're really looking for?" At this point, really ask questions to get the true objection so that you can solve that problem. Most of the time people object, not because they really want an answer but because they want to see how you answer the question or how you react to the question being asked. No matter if someone objects, always make sure to smile, agree with them, and then tell them the truth from your angle.

"That's been one of my mantras – focus and simplicity. Simple can be harder than complex: You have to work hard to get your thinking clean to make it simple. But it's worth it in the end because once you get there, you can move mountains."

STEVE JOBS

(The man who personally led the charge to make personal computers that non-nerds could use, the man who co-founded Apple, the man who introduced the first 100% digitally animated box office success story (Toy Story) when he was the CEO of the company. The man who revolutionized the music industry with the iPod and iTunes. The man who introduced the iPad tablet technology to the planet and the man who introduced the game-changing phone, the iPhone, to the planet. He was a dude who got things done.)

DEEP THOUGHTS FROM THE MATTRESS KING

" "

It doesn't matter what your goal is or what your numbers are; you just need to know those numbers and work backwards. You need to see how many sales you need and how much profit you need in order to make the income that you want to make.

Darren Conrad

CHAPTER 7

DELIVERY & INVENTORY

(GET THE DETAILS RIGHT AND YOU'LL SLEEP TIGHT)

Delivery

If a customer asks if we deliver, I say, "Well, we're not a delivery company, but I have a guy that will bring it to you. He charges $40-$50 for delivery." Having a delivery guy will help you clear out your inventory more quickly. The best way to find a delivery guy is to look for a young kid who is in the lawn care business, landscaping business, or anyone who has a pick up truck. We don't actually employ the delivery people, we just recommend their service. This is exactly the same way Home Depot operates; if someone needs an electrician, Home Depot will suggest a local electrician, but they don't actually employ the electrician. When someone asks us about delivery, we suggest a delivery guy that can transport the mattress to their house, and the customer will then pay the delivery guy directly for the service.

"No one gets good at anything without repetition. Practice, practice, practice and then, when you've begun to master your moves so that you know what to do automatically, it gets exciting. But pigheaded discipline comes first."

CHET HOLMES

(The best-selling author of The Ultimate Sales Machine and the legendary business growth consultant who was personally mentored by Charlie Munger, the long-time business partner of Warren Buffett.)

Inventory

Place orders every week and manage your inventory. The goal each week is to CLEAR OUT everything in your location and purchase new inventory each and every week. This creates a sense of URGENCY in your business process. For example- invest $8,000 each week in inventory and turn it into $12-14K. REPEAT.

"You must take personal responsibility. You cannot change the circumstances, the seasons, or the wind, but you can change yourself. That is something you are in charge of."

JIM ROHN

(The legendary self-help guru, best-selling author and sales trainer who taught millions of people how to become more productive and successful in their lives.)

CHAPTER 8
GROWTH
(THE PATH TO YOUR DREAM WORLD)

Additional Staff

One major benefit of owning and operating the business by yourself is keeping low overhead. Opening up a store and paying someone to run it for you does not work as well as you personally following the business model and turning the inventory yourself. After you've been in the business for a while and you understand the business, you can always bring in someone to help, but I suggest doing it by yourself for the first year so that you can be the most profitable and successful.

"Ideas are easy. Implementation is hard."

GUY KAWASAKI

(Multiple-time www.ThrivetimeShow.com podcast guest, and best-selling author, speaker, entrepreneur and evangelist. He is the chief evangelist of Canva, an online graphic design tool, a brand ambassador for Mercedes-Benz and an executive fellow of the Haas School of Business (UC Berkeley). He was the chief evangelist of Apple and a trustee of the Wikimedia Foundation. He is also the author of The Art of the Start 2.0, The Art of Social Media, Enchantment, and nine other books. Guy earned his Bachelor of Arts from Stanford University and an MBA from UCLA as well as an honorary doctorate from Babson College.)

Time Management

One of the best tips I can give you is to intentionally schedule your work week. Have a weekly schedule for your work week and stick to it. Plan your business week around your life, not your life around your business. I recommend starting your schedule on Sunday and ending on Saturday. Another tip is to schedule your NEW customers, pick-ups and deliveries all in the same three- to four-hour window of time.

"Without a sense of urgency, desire loses its value."

JIM ROHN

(The legendary self-help guru, best-selling author and sales trainer who taught millions of people how to become more productive and successful in their lives.)

Track Your Business

The difference between making $50-$75,000 a year and making $150-$300,000 a year is tracking your business. It can and will increase your profitability and success tremendously. Tracking your business includes elements such as knowing your average profit per transaction, your sales ratio, and your closing ratio, etc.

Earlier in chapter two, I showed a chart of tracking your business in order to know your number and grow your number. Looking at the example in that chart page 58—if you sell 15 mattresses a week at $150 profit, you will make $39,000 a year. An additional ten sales a week at those same numbers (which is just 1.4 extra sales a day) is $117,000. Over the course of a year, that's almost three times the income. The difference is 1.4 extra sales a day.

I can't overemphasize tracking your business on a daily basis. The difference between being super successful or breaking even is so small; you need to know your average profit. As another example using the chart from Chapter 2, if you sell 15 mattresses a week at an average of $250 profit, that's $52,000 a year. But if you sell 25 mattresses a week (which is an extra 1.4 every day), that's $156,000 income. This almost again triples your income.

When you understand your numbers, you can start working backwards. If you want to earn $3,000 a week after expenses, and you know your expenses are $2,500 a week, then you would need to gross $5,500 every week. If you know your average profit is $250 a sale, then you know that you need to make 25 sales a week to reach your goal. It doesn't matter what your goal is or what your numbers are; you just need to know those numbers and work backwards.

You need to see how many sales you need and how much profit you need in order to make the income that you want to make.

Business Profile Page

We have created a simple process on your business profile page where you can input your daily numbers—the number scheduled, the number of shows, the number of sold products, and the total number of profit. Utilizing this page will show you what your weekly average profit is, what your average profit per sale is, your ranking, and your personal records (PR). Your personal records include information such as the most sales you've had in a week, the most sales you've had in a day, the most profit you've had in a week, and the most profit you've had in the day.

This page will also track the number of "Grand Days," which means $1,000 or more of profit in a day. When you make it, you will be a part of the "Grand Day Club." Additionally, there is also a "Consistency Club." Consistency is so important in this business; always remember that this business is a marathon, not a sprint. You will need to do the repeatable, actionable processes to have success on a weekly basis. All of this is available on your dealer page to help you navigate your numbers.

Dashboard
Profile
Weekly Stats
Order Inventory
Events
Showroom Map

		Weekly Profit	Profit/Sale	Ranking	Best Sales/ Week	Best Sales/ Day	Consistency Club	Grand Days Club	Google Reviews
		$24,780	$157	3rd	65	17	3	5	500

Leaderboard — Last 30 days

RANK	NAME	EARNINGS	CHANGE
	Sarah Johnson	$45,280	12.5%
	Michael Chen	$42,150	8.3%
	Justus Weber You	$38,920	5.7%
#4	David Rodriguez	$35,640	2.1%
#5	Lisa Anderson	$33,280	15.8%
#6	James Taylor	$31,560	4.2%
#7	Jennifer Martinez	$29,840	0.6%
#8	Robert Thompson	$28,120	9.6%
#9	Maria Garcia	$26,450	6.4%
#10	William Brown	$24,980	3.1%

Personal Monthly Purchases

Jan	$4.2k
Feb	$3.5k
Mar	$5.2k
Apr	$4.6k
May	$6.1k
Jun	$5.5k

National Monthly Purchases Dealer Average

Jan	$3.8k
Feb	$4.1k
Mar	$4.4k
Apr	$4.2k
May	$4.9k
Jun	$5.1k

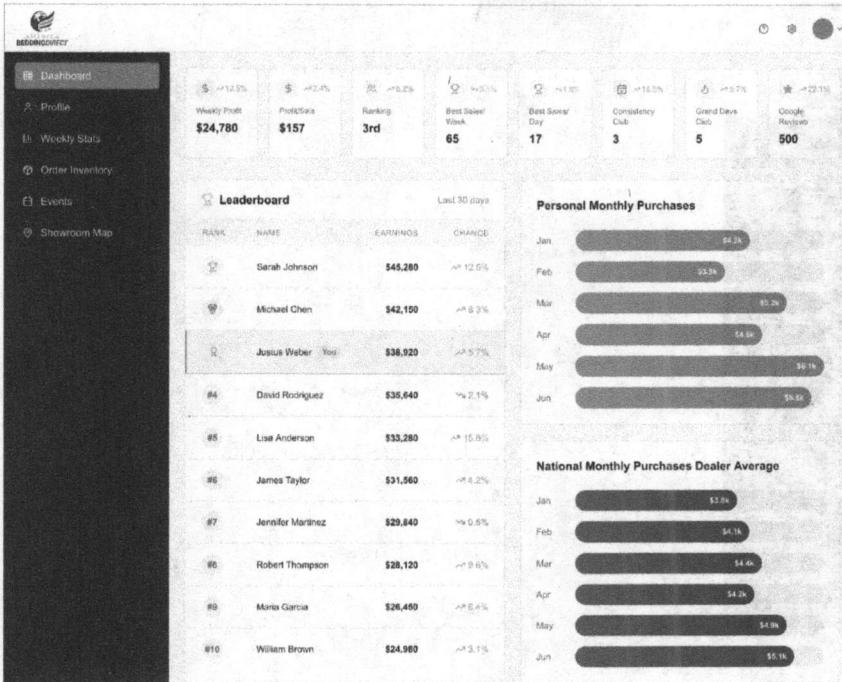

Utilize "Week at a Glance" for your daily results. Using this will help you to react, plan, and proceed successfully. You should know each day's results as well as the accumulative total for the week. These numbers should be listed in your "Week at a Glance." At the end of each day, input your daily results in the weekly stats on your profile page (Scheduled, Show, Sold, Profit & Google Reviews). Add your weekly fixed costs, rent, advertising and coaching.

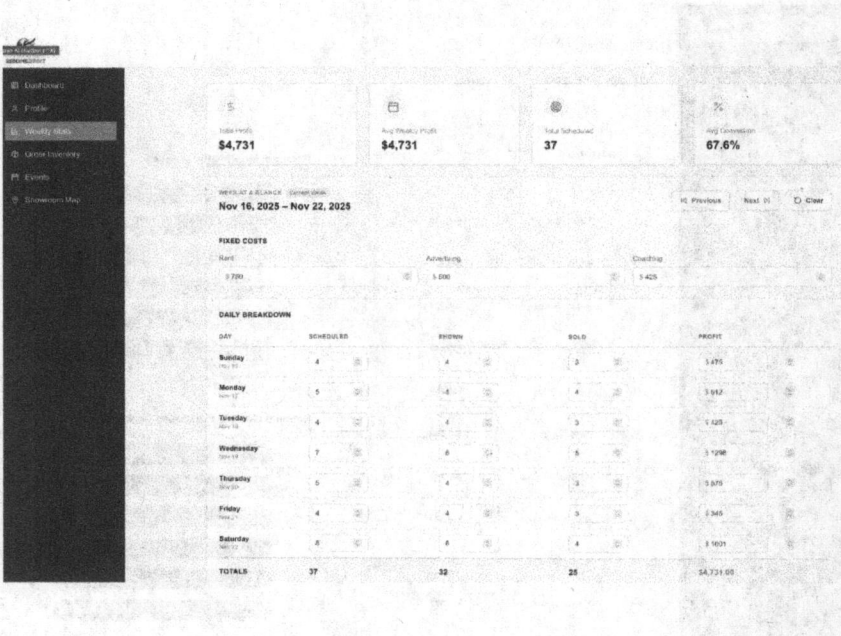

"Don't ever let your business get ahead of the financial side of your business. Accounting, accounting, accounting. Know your numbers."

TILMA FERTITTA

(Tilman Joseph Fertitta (born June 25, 1957) is an American businessman and television personality. He has served as the United States ambassador to Italy and San Marino since May 2025. He is the owner of Landry's and the National Basketball Association (NBA)'s Houston Rockets. Fertitta was the chairman of the board of regents of the University of Houston System from 2014 to 2025.)

"Run your business instead of your business running you"

Create your weekly schedule and be committed to it.

Scheduling process:

Same-day meetings (appointments)—or those booked with less than 1 day of lead time—generally have very low no-show rates compared to longer-lead-time bookings, leading to high show-up percentages. Based on available studies:

> » A 2023 analysis of over 1 million appointments in a large rural U.S. market found a no-show rate of just 2.3% for appointments with (1 day lead time, meaning 97.7% of customers showed up).

> » Scheduling systems, which prioritize same-day or next-day access, consistently reduce overall no-show rates, with same-day bookings often achieving show-up rates above 93% across specialties.

Pick a 3-4 hour window of time each day and set up meetings 15-30 minutes apart.

Take control of your meeting times.

Group people together- it's YOUR time.

Set up meeting times, Do not use the word "Appointment."

Work in pickups around your scheduled meetings.

"If you don't design your own life plan, chances are you'll fall into someone else's plan. And guess what they have planned for you? Not much."

JIM ROHN

(The legendary self-help guru, best-selling author and sales trainer who taught millions of people how to become more productive and successful in their lives.)

Closing Ratio

A good closing ratio for an (appointment) mattress business is generally considered to be between 50% and 70%, but this can vary by industry.

This ratio specifically measures the percentage of appointments that result in a sale, and a consistently low percentage may indicate issues in the sales process.

Factors that can impact closing ratio:

» Sales process: A strong sales process, from initial lead qualification to the final close, is crucial.

» Lead quality: The quality of the leads you are turning into meetings can significantly impact your closing ratio.

» Sales skills: learning to handle objections and nurture leads effectively can improve the outcome of each appointment.

» Industry standards: The "good" closing ratio can vary by industry, but the 50-70% range is a solid target for an appointment-based business model like a mattress store.

Income & Profit

The average profit for an appointment mattress business can range significantly, with conservative estimates suggesting a profit of at least $150 per sale, though many dealers average higher, between $250 and $300 or more.

Profit per sale

» Average profit: A conservative estimate is $150 per sale.

» Higher-end profit: Many dealers average a profit of $250, $300, or more per transaction, but remember it's all about volume. We want to clear everything out, so we give people a great value.

Consistency

This is a very important component of the whole process. We have to be consistent in everything that we do—from our advertising, to our show room set up, to our full approach, to our door greeting, etc. Consistency builds trust. If our ads look like we're clearing out inventory, but our showroom looks like a retail store, that's an inconsistency. If we're trying to create urgency, but our ads make our showroom look like a retail store, that's an inconsistency. Remember, the showroom must look like a clearance center as opposed to a retail store. If our own approach and mannerism doesn't have urgency, that's an inconsistency with our advertising and our showroom set up. So everything must be consistent—from our website, to our social media, to our ads, to our showroom, to our mannerism and demeanor. It all must be consistent and create urgency.

This manual has shown you exactly what you need to do every single step of the way in order to be successful. Our formula is simple and has been used for over three decades. We have mastered this business; all you need to do is plug into our system, follow the guidance we offer, and be teachable. We provide all the resources you need to be successful, and we have provided easy-to-follow instructions to guide you through each aspect of the business.

1. **Advertise** to generate mass amounts of contacts!

2. **Respond** to customers to set up a meeting.

3. **Greet** the customer at the door and recreate the sense of urgency.

4. **TRACK** your business daily.

Keys to Success in the Mattress Business

» Advertise, Advertise, Advertise!

» Read & follow this book.

» Utilize Clay Clark's business coaching system.

» Attend business conferences.

» Stay in contact with other successful dealers weekly.

The Biblical Ten Commandments
(Found In Exodus Chapter 20: 3-17):

Commandment #1 - [3] Thou shalt have no other gods before me. [4] Thou shalt not make unto thee any graven image, or any likeness of any thing that is in heaven above, or that is in the earth beneath, or that is in the water under the earth. [5] Thou shalt not bow down thyself to them, nor serve them: for I the Lord thy God am a jealous God, visiting the iniquity of the fathers upon the children unto the third and fourth generation of them that hate me; [6] And shewing mercy unto thousands of them that love me, and keep my commandments.

Commandment #2 - [7] Thou shalt not take the name of the Lord thy God in vain; for the Lord will not hold him guiltless that taketh his name in vain.

Commandment #3 - [8] Remember the sabbath day, to keep it holy.

Commandment #4 - [9] Six days shalt thou labour, and do all thy work: [10] But the seventh day is the sabbath of the Lord thy God: in it thou shalt not do any work, thou, nor thy son, nor thy daughter, thy manservant, nor thy maidservant, nor thy cattle, nor thy stranger that is within thy gates: [11] For in six days the Lord made heaven and earth, the sea, and all that in them is, and rested the seventh day: wherefore the Lord blessed the sabbath day, and hallowed it.

Commandment #5 - [12] Honour thy father and thy mother: that thy days may be long upon the land which the Lord thy God giveth thee.

Commandment #6 - [13] Thou shalt not kill.

Commandment #7 - [14] Thou shalt not commit adultery.

Commandment #8 - [15] Thou shalt not steal.

Commandment #9 - [16] Thou shalt not bear false witness against thy neighbour.

Commandment #10 - [17] Thou shalt not covet thy neighbour's house, thou shalt not covet thy neighbour's wife, nor his manservant, nor his maidservant, nor his ox, nor his ass, nor any thing that is thy neighbour's.

The American Bedding Direct 10 Commandments for Achieving Success:

Commandment #1 - Thou shall take responsibility for the success or failure of your business.

Commandment #2 - Thou shall urgently secure a commercial location for your business.

Commandment #3 - Thou shall urgently register a Google Map within your local designated market area.

Commandment #4 - Thou shall gather two times more objective Google reviews than any of the local mattress business competitors within your designated market area.

Commandment #5 - Thou shall diligently meet with your business coach each week to learn what action items you need to take to earn the money you want to make.

Commandment #6 - Thou shall block out the time needed to turn your to-do list into a to-done list.

Commandment #7 - Thou shall gather two times more objective Google reviews than any of the local mattress business competitors within your designated market area.

Commandment #8 - Thou shall measure what you treasure and track where you don't want your business to slack.

Commandment #9 - Thou shall call, text and email your leads until they cry, buy or die.

Commandment #10 - Thou shall gather two times more objective Google reviews than any of the local mattress business competitors within your designated market area.

Bonus Chapter

FIND THOUSANDS OF REAL CLAY CLARK CLIENT SUCCESS STORIES AT
THRIVETIMESHOW.COM/TESTIMONIALS

Barbee Cookies
Kat Graham
www.BarbeeCookies.com
2014 - 2015 Up 140%
Industry - Bakery

Best Buy Window Treatment
Ergun Aral
www.BestBuyWindowTreatments.com
2018 - 2019 Up 76%
Industry - Window Treatments

Bigfoot Restoration
Marc Lucero & Stephen Small
www.BigFootRestoration.com
2018 - 2019 Up 112%
Industry - Disaster
Restoration and Repair

Bogard and Sons Construction
Andy Bogard
www.BogardandSons.com
2018 - 2019 Up 32%
Industry - Home Building
and Remodeling

Breakout Creative
Chris De Jesus
www.BreakOutCreativeCompany.com
Up 59% Total
Industry - Advertising
Brian T. Armstrong
Construction Incorporated
Brian T. Armstrong

2017 - 2018 Up 29%
2018 - 2019 Up 89%
Industry - Home Builder

C&R Contracting
Ryan Kilday
www.ColoradoContracting.com
2018 - 2019 Up 240%
Industry - Contracting and Remodeling

Catalyst Communication
Adam Duran
www.
CatalystCommunicationsGroupInc.com
2018 - 2019 Up 44%
Industry - Commercial Security Systems

Chaney Construction
Jim and Amy Chaney
www.ChaneyConstructionTX.com
2018 - 2019 Up 19%
Industry - Home Builder

Citywide Mechanical
Terrance Thomas
www.CityWide-Mechanical.com
2018 - 2019 Up 118%
Industry - Heating and Air
CK Electric
Chad Kudlacek
www.CKElectricOmaha.com
2018 - 2019 Up 25%
Industry - Electrician

Colaw Fitness
Charles and Amber Colaw
www.ColawFitness.com
2018 - 2019 Up 15%
Industry - Fitness Gym

Compass Roofing
Robert Alsbrooks & Sonny Ordonez
www.CompassRoofing.com
2018 - 2019 Up 103%
Industry - Commercial and
Residential Roofing

Complete Carpet
Nathan & Toni Sevrinus
www.CompleteCarpetTulsa.com
2017 - 2019 Up 298%
Industry - Carpet Cleaning

Comfort Pro
Steve Bagwell
www.ComfortPro-Inc.com
2018 - 2019 Up 28%
Industry - Heating and Air

CT Tech
Christopher Tracy
https://cttec.net/
2018 - 2019 Up 77%
Industry - IT Support

Curtis Music
Ron Curtis
www.CurtisMusicAcademy.com
2018 - 2019 Up 58%
Industry - Music Teacher

Custom Automation
Technologies Incorporated
Dan Hoehnen
www.CustomAutomationTech.com
2018 - 2019 Up 16%
Industry - Custom Automation

D&D Custom Homes
Dave Tucker
www.MidSouthHomeBuilder.com
2018 - 2019 Up 45%
Industry - Custom Home Builder

Da Vinci
Josh Fellman and Jerome Garrett
www.500KMSP.com
2018 - 2019 Up 1,097%
Managed Service Provider Consulting

Danco
Denise Richter
www.DancoPump.com
2018 - 2019 Up 17%
Industry - manufacturing
and distribution

Delricht Research
Tyler and Rachel Hastings
www.DelrichtResearch.com
2018 - 2019 Up 300%
Industry - Clinical Research

Dr. Breck Kasbaum Chiropractor
Dr. Breck Kasbaum
www.DrBreck.com
2018 - 2019 Up 50%
Industry - Chiropractic

Duct Armor
Tim Borgne
https://www.ductarmor.com/
2015 - 2016 Up 20%
Industry - Air Duct Repair

Dynamic Electrical So
Edward Durant
www.DynaElec.com
2018 - 2019 Up 16%
Industry - Electrician

ECS Electric
James Crews
www.ECSElectricllc.com
2018 - 2019 Up 26%
Industry - Electrician

Edmond Dental
Dr. Joseph Tucker
www.EdmondDentalatDeerCreek.com
2018 - 2019 Up 205%
Industry - Dentist

Electrical Investments
James Henry
www.ElectricalInvestments.com
2018 - 2019 Up 21%
Industry - Electrician

EnviZion Insurance
Austin Grieci
www.EZInsurancePlan.com
2018 - 2019 Up 800%
Industry - Auto Insurance

Full Package Media
Thomas James Crosson
www.FullPackageMedia.com
2018 - 2019 Up 15%
Commercial Real Estate Photography

Gable's Excavating Incorporated
Levi Gable
www.GEI-USA.com
2018 - 2019 Up 66%
Industry - Utility Contractor

The Garage
Roy Coggeshall
www.TheGarageBA.com
2018 - 2019 Up 19%
2017 - Present Up 70%
Industry - Auto Repair

The Grill Gun
Bob Healey
www.GrillBlazer.com
From Idea to Manufactured Product
8,725 Funders
Raised $920,009.00 Crowd
Funding the Invention
Industry - Retail Products

H2Oasis Float Center
Debra Worthington
www.H2OasisFloatCenter.com
Up 17% Total
Industry - Float Therapy

Handy Bros Services
David Visser
www.HandyBros-Services.com
2018 - 2019 Up 136%
Industry - Handyman

HealthRide
Ryan Graff
www.HealthRideTulsa.org
2018 - 2019 Up 10%
Industry - Non-Emergency
Medical Transportation

Healthworks Chiropractic
Jay Schroeder
www.HealthworksChiropractic.net
2018 - 2019 Up 24%
Industry - Chiropractic
Hood and Associates CPA's, PC

Paul Hood
www.HoodCPAs.com
2018 - 2019 Up 61%
Industry - Accountant

The Hub Gym
Luke Owens
www.TheHubGym.com
2018 - 2019 Up 66.38%
Industry - Fitness Gym

Impressions Painting
Manuel Mora
www.ImpressionsPaintingTulsa.com
2018 - 2019 Up 41%
Industry - House Painting

Inspired Spaces
Josh Fellman and Jerome Garrett
www.InspiredSpacesOK.com
2018 - 2019 Up 40%
Industry - Epoxy Flooring

Jameson Fine Cabinetry
Jamie Fagel
www.JamesonFineCabinetry.com
2018 - 2019 Up 31%
Industry - Home Improvement

Jean Briese
Jean Briese
www.JeanBriese.com
2018 - 2019 Up 90%
4. Motivational Speaker

KAE Edward Plumbing
Ron & Jacqueline Mader
www.KaeEdwardPlumbing.com
2018 - 2019 Up 46%
Industry - Plumber

Kelly Construction Group
Jon Kelly
www.KellyConstructionGroup.com
2018 - 2019 Up 42%
Industry - General Contractor

Kona Honu
Byron Kay
www.KonaHonuDivers.com
2018 - 2019 Up 14%
Industry - Diving Tours and
Scuba Instruction

Kurb to Kitchen
Lonny & Rinda Myers
www.KurbtoKitchenLLC.com
2018 - 2019 Up 126%
Industry - Home Remodeling

Kvell Fitness & Nutrition
Brett Denton
www.KvellFit.com
2018-2019 Up 35%+
Industry - Fitness Gym

Lake Martin Mini Mall
Jason Lett
www.LakeMartinCubed.com
2018 - $685,804.00
2019 - $782,551.00
14% Growth
Industry - Retail Products

Lakeshore Plumbing
Mike Boulte
www.LakeShorePlumbingOKC.com
2018 - 2019 Up 100%
Industry - Plumber

Laundry Barn
Josh Fellman
www.TheLaundryBarn.com
2018 - 2019 Up 100%
Industry - Laundromat

Living Water Irrigation
Josh Wilson
www.LivingWaterIrrigationOK.com
2017 - 2019 Up 600%
Industry - Sprinkler Install

Mennis Heating
Mike Ennis
www.MennisHeatingandCooling.com
2018 - 2019 Up 400%
Industry - Heating and Air

Metal Roof Contractors
Doug Yarholar
www.MetalRoofContractorsOK.com
2018 - 2019 Up 14%
Industry - Metal Roof Contractor

Mod Scenes
Steven Hall
www.ModScenes.com
2018 - 2019 Up 83%
Industry - Stage Design

Morrow, Lai and Kitterman
Pediatric Dentistry
Dr. Mark Morrow, Dr. April Lai,
and Dr. Kerry Kitterman
www.MLKDentistry.com
2018 - 2019 Up 42%
Industry - Dentist

Mr. Rooter
Joshua Creasy
www.MrRooter.com/New-Braunfels/
2018 - 2019 Up 75%
Industry - Plumber

Multi-Clean
Kevin Thomas
www.MultiCleanOK.com
2018 - 2019 Up 14%
Industry - Commercial Cleaning

OK Roof Nerds
Marty Grisham
www.OKRoofNerds.com
2018 - 2019 Up 74%
Industry - Commercial and
Residential Roofer

One Way Plumbing
Chad Ward
www.OneWayPlumbing.biz
2018 - 2019 Up 11%
Industry - Plumbing

Oxi Fresh
Jonathan Barnett
Matt Kline - Franchise Developer
www.OxiFresh.com
2007 to 2019 - 400 Locations Opened
Industry - Carpet Cleaning

Pappagallo's Pizza
Dave Rich
www.Pappagallos.com
2018 - 2019 Up 21%
Industry - Restaurant

Platinum Pest
Jennifer and Jared Johnson
www.PlatinumPestandLawn.com
2018-2019 - 25% Growth
2017-2018 - 43% Growth
Industry - Pest Control

PMH OKC
Randy Antrikan
www.PMHOKC.com
2018 - 2019 Up 70%
Industry - Outdoor Living
/ Retail Products

Precision Calibration
Nathan Saylor
www.PrecisionCalibrations.com
2018 - 2019 Up 62%
Industry - Equipment Calibration

Quality Surfaces
John Cook
www.QualitySurfacesIn.com
2018 - 2019 Up 84%
Industry - Commercial and
Residential Remodeling

RC Auto Specialists
Roy Coggeshall
www.RCAutoSpecialists.com
2018 - 2019 Up 9%
Industry - Auto Repair

Rescue Roofer TX
Wesley Cannon
www.RoofingDenton.com
2018 - 2019 Up 79%
Industry - Commercial and
Residential Roofer

Revitalize Medical Spa
Lindsey Blankenship and Crista Hobbs
www.RevitalizeMedicalSpa.com
2018 - 2019 Up 36%
Industry - Medical Cosmetics

Roofing & Siding Smiths
Zach Potts
www.RoofingandSidingSmiths.com
2018 - 2019 Up 67%
Industry - Roofing and Siding

Rogers Plumbing
Roger Patterson
https://plumberinaustin.com
2018 - 2019 Up 33%
Industry - Plumber

Scotch Construction
Tim Scotch
www.ScotchConstruction.com
2017 - 2019 Up 492%
Industry - Home Builder

Shaw Homes
Aaron Antis
www.ShawHomes.com
2018 - 2019 Up 116%
Industry - Custom Home Builder

Sierra Pools
Cody Albright
www.SierraPoolsandSpas.com
2017 - 2019 Up 309%
Industry - Pool Construction

Snow Bear Air
Daniel Ramos
www.SnowBearAir.com
2018 - 2019 Up 41%
Industry - Heating and Air

Southeastern Computer Associates
Ben Miner
https://sca-atl.com/
2018 - $2,011,394.51 -
2019 - $5,531,144.01
Industry - IT Support

Spot-On Plumbing
Brandon Brown
www.SpotOnPlumbingTulsa.com
2018 - 2019 Up 120%
Industry - Plumber

Spurrell & Associates Chartered
Professional Accountants
Josh Spurrell
www.Spurrell.ca
2018 - 2019 Up 50%
Industry - Accounting

Struct Construction
Brandon Haaga
www.StructConstruction.com
2018 - 2019 Up 60%
Industry - Construction Contractor

Tesla Electric
Felix Keil
www.TeslaElectricColorado.com
2018 - 2019 Up 60%
Industry - Tesla Electric

Tip Top K9
Ryan and Rachel Wimpey
www.TipTopK9.com
1 Location - 10 Locations
Industry - Dog Training

Trinity Employment
Cory Minter
www.TrinityEmployment.com
2018-2019 Up 35%
Industry - Staffing

Turley Solutions & Innovations
Rance Turley
www.TSI.lc
2018 - 2019 Up 300%
Industry - IT Support

Tuscaloosa Ophthalmology
Doctor Timothy Johnson
www.TTownEyes.com
2018 - 2019 Up 16%
Industry - Doctor

Viva Med
Chris Lacroix
www.MyVivaMed.com
2018 - 2019 Up 90%
Industry - Primary Care Physicians

Veteran Home Exterior
James Peterson
www.VeteranHomeExterior.com
2018 - 2019 Up 145%
Industry - Window Replacement

White Glove Auto
Myron Kirkpatrick
WhiteGloveAutoTulsa.com
2018 - 2019 - 27%
Industry - Auto Detailing

Williams Contracting
Travis Williams
www.Will-Con.com
2018 - 2019 Up 33%
Industry - Construction Management

Witness Security
Keith Schultz
www.WitnessLLC.com
2017 - 2019 Up 300%
Industry - Home Security Systems

"ACTA NON VERBA is the motto of the U.S. Merchant Marine Academy. Don't listen to what a person says, watch what they do."

- *Robert Kiyosaki*

(An international best-selling author of the Rich Dad Poor Dad book series, a legendary real estate investor, multiple-time ThrivetimeShow.com podcast guest, and entrepreneur. Kiyosaki is the author of more than 26 books, including the international self-published personal finance Rich Dad Poor Dad series of books which has been translated into 51 languages and sold over 41 million copies worldwide.)

Money Is Simply a Magnifier (Both Good and Bad):

Money is just a magnifier, and I have consistently found that teaching YOU how to make more money and how to create both time and financial freedom simply allows YOU to become more of who YOU are, both GOOD and BAD.

If you are generous, having increased financial means will allow you to give even more to help those in need. If you like going out to eat, with additional income you will have the financial resources to NOW go out to eat more often. If you love traveling, with financial abundance in your wallet, you will be able to travel even more. With additional cash in the bank, if you are excited about buying exotic cars, having increased financial resources will allow you to buy even more exotic cars because money is just a magnifier. However, it is my sincere and highest desire that I haven't taught you the proven processes and success strategies so that you can become a MASSIVE ASS because the world already has enough of those (Mark Zuckerberg, Jack Dorsey, Bill Gates, etc.)

> "[36] For what shall it profit a man, if he shall gain the whole world, and lose his own soul?"
>
> **MARK 8:36**
> *KJV*

So as we complete this workbook (and potentially this workshop) together, I would encourage you to sit down with yourself, with your spouse and with GOD'S PLAN FOR YOUR LIFE firmly placed in your mind and I would ask yourself the following question.

If you had all of the money in the world what goals would you have for your faith, family, finances, fitness, friendship, fun, and focus.

I would encourage you to take 30 minute to actually sketch out your ideal calendar in a perfect world where you have the financial freedom and time freedom needed to dictate what you will do with your days and whom you will spend your time with. Don't mail it in here. This is the entire point of learning how to grow a successful business. Fill in the calendar below the time that you will devote to your faith, your family, your finances, your fitness, your friend and your pursuit of fun. Don't be afraid to schedule guitar lessons, workouts, time to take your kids camping or that all important trip that you've been putting off. Every day that we are given on this planet is a gift from our God above, however what we do with each and every day is our gift to God. Remember being present is a present. But, remember, only what gets scheduled gets done.

"THE SECRET TO BUYING LAMBORGHINI'S"

Step 1: Follow Clay Clark's systems

Step 2: Buy Lamborghini's

"I own 6 Lamborghini's."

- STEVE CURRINGTON
Mortgage Broker
SteveCurrington.com

WANT TO KNOW EVEN MORE?
CHECK OUT ALL OF CLAY'S BOOKS AT
THRIVETIMESHOW.COM/FREE-RESOURCES

HOW TO BUILD A SUCCESSFUL BUSINESS
The World's Best Business Growth & Consulting Book: Business Growth Strategies from the World's Best Business Coach.

PODCAST DOMINATION 101
This book will show you how to prepare, record, launch, and begin generating income from your podcast, all from your home studio!

TRADE-UPS
Learn how to design and live the life you love, how to find and create the time needed to get things done in a world filled with endless digital distractions, and more!

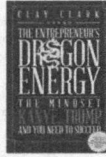

THE ENTREPRENEUR'S DRAGON ENERGY
The Mindset Kanye, Trump and You Need to Succeed.

THRIVE
How to Take Control of Your Destiny and Move Beyond Surviving... Now!

JACKASSARY
Jackassery will serve as a beacon of light for other entrepreneurs that are looking to avoid troublesome employees and difficult situations. This is real. This is raw. This is unfiltered entrepreneurship.

BOOM
The 14 Proven Steps to Business Success.

SEARCH ENGINE DOMINATION
Learn the Proven System We've Used to Earn Millions.

FEAR UNMASKED
Fear Unmasked gives you the essential information you need to know about the coronavirus, the government shutdown, and the media that is perpetuating the hysteria.

IT'S NOT LONELY AT THE TOP
15 Keys to achieving a successful, peaceful, and drama-free life. (3/4 of this book is handwritten by Clay Clark, himself).

HOW TO REPEL FRIENDS AND NOT INFLUENCE PEOPLE
The epic whale of a tale featuring America's self proclaimed most humble male.

HOW TO BUILD A SUCCESSFUL BUSINESS
In This Game Changing & Life Changing Book You Will Learn the Proven Processes, Success Strategies, and Secrets to Unlocking Your Potential While Learning the Following & More:

HOW TO BUILD A SUCCESSFUL BUSINESS
In This Game Changing & Life Changing Book You Will Learn the Proven Processes, Success Strategies, and Secrets to Unlocking Your Potential While Learning the Following & More:

FEAR UNMASKED 2.0
Updated and revised for 2021. Fear Unmasked 2.0 provides more resources to kill the spirit of fear and giving YOU an action plan to save America.

BELICHICK: AN UNAUTHORIZED LOOK UNDER THE HOODIE
Many fans enthusiastically cheer for the EPIC teams assembled and coached by Coach Bill Belichick.

CREATING HABITUAL WEALTH
Learn the proven path to creating financial success.

F6 JOURNAL
Meta Thrive Time Journal.

FEAR UNMASKED
Fear Unmasked gives you the essential information you need to know about the coronavirus, the government shutdown, and the media that is perpetuating the hysteria.

HOW TO BECOME SUSTAINABLY RICH
In This Game Changing & Life Changing Book You Will Learn the Proven Processes, Success Strategies, and Secrets to Unlocking Your Potential While Learning the Following & More:

WILL NOT WORK FOR FOOD
9 Big Ideas for Effectively Managing Your Business in an Increasingly Dumb, Distracted & Dishonest America.

THE ART OF POWERFUL PUBLIC SPEAKING
In this page-turning power-packed classic, Clay Clark teams up with the (now deceased) long-time friend and speaking mentor Carlton Pearson to teach you proven public speaking tips, tricks, and moves that you can use.

SALES DOMINATION
Clay Clark is a master of selling and now he wants to teach you his proven processes, scalable systems and sales mastery moves in a humorous and practical way.

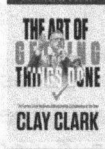

THE ELEPHANT IN THE ROOM
In this action-focused guide, Clay Clark gives you a proven plan to fast-track you to success!

THE ART OF GETTING THINGS DONE
Clay Clark breaks down the proven, time-tested and time freedom creating super moves that you can use to create both the time freedom and financial freedom that most people only dream about.

THE HOMO DEUCE
This book was written to provide you with a POWERFUL TOOL to help you wake up your family and friends to "The Great Reset" and "Fourth Industrial Revolution" agenda

WHEEL OF WEALTH
An Entrepreneur's Action Guide.

MAKE YOUR LIFE EPIC
Clay shares his journey and struggle from the dorm room to the board room during his raw and action-packed story of how he built DJConnection.com.

HOW TO HIRE QUALITY EMPLOYEES
This candid book shares how to avoid being held hostage by employees.

THE GREAT RESET VERSUS THE GREAT AWAKENING
The Great Reset Versus The Great Awakening breaks down this EPIC battle between good and evil.

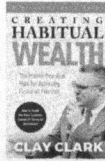

IF MY WALLS COULD TALK
The Notes, Quotes, & Epiphanies I've Written On Clay's Office Walls. (Hardcover).

"Vision without execution is just hallucination."

- Thomas Edison
(The man who invented the modern light bulb, recorded audio, recorded video and the founder of GE)

"Before success comes in any man's life, he's sure to meet with much temporary defeat and, perhaps, some failures. When defeat overtakes a man, the easiest and the most logical thing to do is to quit. That's exactly what the majority of men do."

- Napoleon Hill
(The best-selling author of Think and Grow Rich. I named my son Aubrey Napoleon-Hill Clark after Napoleon-Hill because Napoleon Hill's research, teaching and writing had such a profound impact on me and my wife.)

BONUS CHAPTER

20 SUPER MOVES You Can Use to Build Your Reputation and DRAMATICALLY Increase Your Compensation + Quotable Claymations

"No one lives long enough to learn everything they need to learn starting from scratch. To be successful, we absolutely, positively have to find people who have already paid the price to learn the things that we need to learn to achieve our goals."

- Brian Tracy
(The legendary best-selling author, sales trainer, business growth consultant and keynote success speaker)

Super Move #1
STOP HANGING AROUND IDIOTS

You must accept that you will become the average of the five people that you spend the most time with. You must understand that becoming successful is not normal and that most people are wrong about most things most of the time, including:

"He that walketh with wise men shall be wise: but a companion of fools shall be destroyed."
- Proverbs 10:4

Super Move #2
CARRY A TO-DO LIST AT ALL TIMES

When you don't carry a to-do list, it becomes very easy to waste your time doing things that don't matter and you become known as the person who is forgetful, unreliable, and untrustworthy. If your desire is to be promoted, you must up your game when it comes to becoming an organized and proactive person. Every day before you see another human, it is essential that you create a to-do list with your daily action items on it.

☺ **FUN FACT:**
"U.S. adults now spend nearly half a day interacting with media. American adults spend over 11 hours per day listening to, watching, reading or generally interacting with media." - https://www.nielsen.com/insights/2018/time-flies-us-adults-now-spend-nearly-half-a-day-interacting-with-media/

Super Move #3

CARRY A PRINTED VERSION OF TODAY'S CALENDAR AT ALL TIMES

As you move up, you will have more and more responsibilities put on your plate. In order to not forget something important, it is imperative for your success that you carry a printed copy of your calendar at all times. As an example, I sincerely have no idea what I am supposed to do tomorrow, but my calendar knows, thus, I print it off daily.

"What gets scheduled gets done."

- Lee Cockerell
(The former Executive Vice President of Walt Disney World Resorts who once managed over 40,000 cast members / employees)

Super Move #4
DON'T HAVE SEX WITH SOMEONE YOU JUST MET

Over the years, I have personally watched people throw their entire careers away for a regrettable and passionate night with someone they just met. Soon, they find out that they have a disease or a child on the way, and they begin to find their lives filled with chaos. When in doubt, don't have sex with someone you just met. Know where you are going and go there and avoid lascivious people that are drifting sexually.

"The world has the habit of making room for the man whose actions show that he knows where he is going"

- Napoleon Hill
(The best-selling author of Think & Grow Rich. The book Think & Grow Rich changed my life and I named my son after him, Aubrey Napoleon-Hill Clark.)

Super Move #5
ALWAYS KNOW YOUR GOALS

When you go out of your way to always be in tune and aware of the company's goals, you are setting yourself apart from most employees who simply came to work for a check. When you know the company's goals, you will find yourself coming up with new ideas to make the company more efficient and more profitable.

THE CAPACITY OF TENACITY:
OVERCOMING OBSTACLES

"Only the paranoid survive."

- Andy Grove
(Under Andy Grove's leadership, Intel became the world's largest chip maker and one of the most admired companies in the world. In Only the Paranoid Survive, Grove reveals his strategy for measuring the nightmare moment every leader dreads--when massive change occurs and a company must, virtually overnight, adapt or fall by the wayside--in a new way.)

Super Move #7

VIEW WORK AS "WORSHIP" AND NOT JUST AS A JOB

The Old Testament of the Bible was written in Hebrew. In Hebrew, the word "work" and the word "worship" mean the same thing. Thus, when God told Adam to "work in the garden", he was telling Adam that his work ethic was the best way for Adam to give praise and "worship" to his creator. In order to achieve his massive success, you must learn how to view your "work" as your "worship."

To learn more about this concept, listen to my interviews with Rabbi Daniel Lapin: https://www.thrivetimeshow.com/podcast-guests/rabbi-daniel-lapin/

Super Move #8

If you want to get promoted, you need to get noticed (for doing the right things). You simply cannot just show up to work on time and do your job and expect to get that job promotion you've been looking for. In order to get that promotion, you have to get your boss's attention. When you exceed your clients expectations, you will WOW them.

"If you're remarkable, it's likely that some people won't like you. That's part of the definition of remarkable. Nobody gets unanimous praise—ever. The best the timid can hope for is to be unnoticed. Criticism comes to those who stand out."

- Seth Godin
(Born in 1977, Godin worked at a bagel factory that produced everything bagels. After leaving Spinnaker in 1986, he used $20,000 in savings to establish Seth Godin Productions, which primarily operated as a book packaging business. He operated this venture out of a studio apartment in New York City. He then met Mark Hurst and founded Yoyodyne (named in jest after the fictional Yoyodyne in The Adventures of Buckaroo Banzai Across the 8th Dimension. In 1998, he sold Yoyodyne to Yahoo! for about $30 million.)

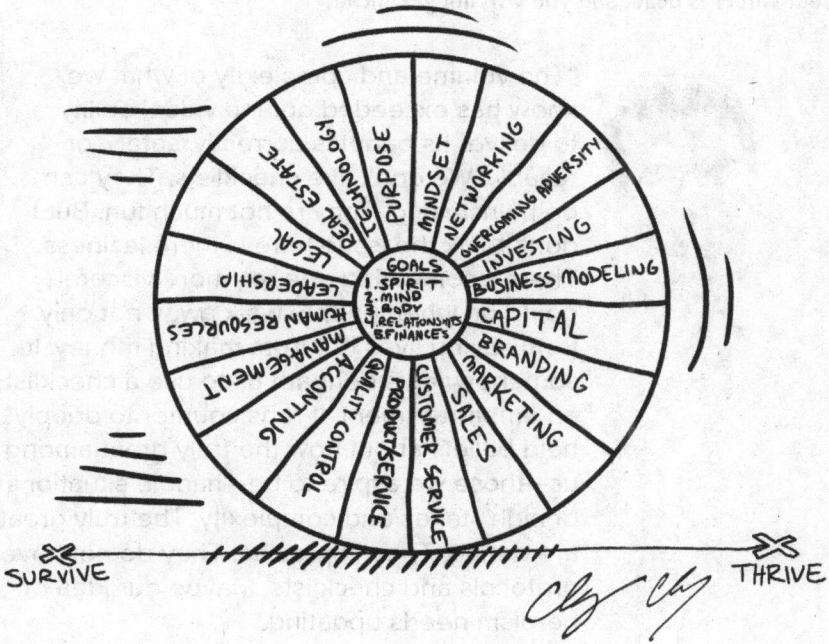

THE WHEEL OF WEALTH
DON'T REINVENT THE WHEEL

SURVIVE — THRIVE

Use the proven processes, success strategies and time-tested systems.

Super Move #9

TURN IN ALL PROJECTS EARLY AND USE CHECKLISTS FOR EVERYTHING

When you commit to turning in all work projects early, you get known as a person that can be counted on and that is powerful. When you turn in projects on time or barely on time, you are not standing out and you are not going in the right direction if your goal is winning at work. If you miss deadlines, your career is dead, and you will not get ahead.

"The volume and complexity of what we know has exceeded our individual ability to deliver its benefits correctly, safely, or reliably. We don't like checklists. They can be painstaking. They're not much fun. But I don't think the issue here is mere laziness. There's something deeper, more visceral going on when people walk away not only from saving lives but from making money. It somehow feels beneath us to use a checklist, an embarrassment. It runs counter to deeply held beliefs about how the truly great among us—those we aspire to be—handle situations of high stakes and complexity. The truly great are daring. They improvise. They do not have protocols and checklists. Maybe our idea of heroism needs updating."

- Atul Gawande

(The best-selling author of The Checklist Manifesto: How to Get Things Right, a renowned surgeon, writer, and public health leader. Prior to joining the Biden-Harris administration, he was a practicing general and endocrine surgeon at Brigham and Women's Hospital and a professor at Harvard Medical School and the Harvard T.H. Chan School of Public Health.)

Super Move #10
BRING GREAT ENERGY TO WORK

Nobody wants to work with a "mopey" person and "whiny" person. Customers don't want to buy from low-energy people. Employees don't want to be managed by negative and angry bosses. Volunteers cannot be inspired by passionless leaders. If you want to succeed, you must dig deep down and find that great energy every day before you come into the workplace.

"You can start right where you stand and apply the habit of going the extra mile by rendering more service and better service than you are now being paid for."

- Napoleon Hill

(A man who was mentored directly by the steel tycoon Andrew Carnegie, the best-selling self-help author of all-time during his lifetime, the author of Think & Grow Rich, The Law of Success, The Master-Key to Riches, etc...)

Super Move #11

DETERMINE TO BE IN THE TOP 5% OF YOUR INDUSTRY

Regardless of what the coworkers around you are up to, YOU must focus on becoming the best "YOU" can be. Don't worry or even think about the people around you that might be "mailing it in", and "doing just enough to not get fired". You personally must focus on being in the top 5% of your industry. How can you get better? How can you improve your performance?

Super Move #12

WEAR A SMILE ALL DAY

....

When you look pissed, you repel promotions and opportunities. No matter what you are going through, make it your mission to keep your face in the happy optimistic position. A smile says to the world, "I am looking for promotion, success, and to be my best." A frown or the absence of a smile says "Stay away from me. What I have might be contagious."

"About half of the salespeople I've worked with over the years gave up after a single rejection. They would call a client, the client would say no, and the salesperson would never call that person back. Very few, perhaps only 4 percent to 5 percent, keep trying after four rejections. Yet, as you learned in the previous chapter, I've found that it takes about 8.4 rejections to get a meeting. And what makes the difference between people who will face that rejection one time and quit or 40 times and never quit is determined purely by the strength of their ego."

- Chet Holmes

(The iconic sales trainer, business growth consultant and the best-selling author of The Ultimate Sales Machine: Turbocharge Your Business with Relentless Focus on 12 Key Strategies)

Super Move #13
BECOME A NOTE-TAKER

If your quest is to be the best, you must begin taking notes. Good bosses are busy and top-level managers are always fast-moving, thus, they do not like to have to repeat themselves. When your boss speaks, take notes and write down what they are saying so that you don't have to ask them the same thing repeatedly.

Super Move #14
LEAVE YOUR PERSONAL PROBLEMS AT HOME

We all have personal problems. In the past 10 years, my wife and I have dealt with a miscarriage, the death of close family, cancer in the family, and losing my dad to the ravages of Lougheig's disease, but we don't use these events and unfortunate situations to justify missing work, payroll, etc. No matter what is happening in your personal life, do your job.

THE WEATHER CHANNEL UNPLUGGED:
LET GO OF WHAT YOU CAN'T CONTROL

Super Move #15

ONLY FOCUS ON WOWING YOUR BOSS AND THE CLIENTS

If you want to dominate at work, you must focus on only wowing your boss and your customers. Your coworkers are going to try and distract you, annoy you, and even sabotage you. However, if you will focus on just wowing your boss and your customers, you will win. Don't try to wow all your co-workers and your boss because it is not possible.

"There is one quality which one must possess to win, and that is definiteness of purpose, the knowledge of what one wants, and a burning desire to possess it."

- Napoleon Hill
(Best-selling author of Think and Grow Rich and the former speech writer to President Franklin Delano Roosevelt)

Super Move #16
ENERGIZE AND ENCOURAGE THE PEOPLE AROUND YOU

It only takes a few quick seconds, but bosses notice the employee who compliments and encourages those around them. Take a moment each day and write down something positive and sincere to say about the team members around you. When the time is appropriate, compliment the people around you and cheer for their success.

Super Move #17
BECOME KNOWN AS AN ORGANIZED PERSON

When you are an organized person you cause your boss to trust you. When you are always scrounging around looking for that "thing," and trying to find that "piece of paper" that has all the passwords on it, you will quickly become written off as an unpromotable person. Stay organized and you will find yourself on the path to promotion.

"Genius is 1 percent inspiration, and 99 percent perspiration."

- *Thomas Edison*
(The legendary inventor whose team created the first practical light bulb, the first recorded audio, and the motion picture technology while creating General Electric)

Super Move #18

ASK YOUR BOSS WHAT BOOKS TO READ (AND READ THEM)

You will become the average of the 5 people you spend the most time with and your mindset will be greatly impacted by the books you read. Ask your boss what business books have impacted their career and life the most and then read those books. Apply the principles found within those books and you will win.

"To know thyself is the beginning of wisdom."

- Socrates
(A classical Greek philosopher who was credited as being one of the founders of modern Western Philosophy.)

Super Move #19

GET ENOUGH SLEEP

When you come to work looking like death, that is not a "good look."

Everyone around you will come up to you and ask "Karl, what's wrong?" and "Janet, what's going on? Are you ok?"

People cannot stand employees who always come to work looking "rough". To succeed, you need energy. Turn off Netflix, Amazon video streaming, your video games, and go to bed by 10 PM.

Super Move #20
BE FUNNY (OR AT LEAST ATTEMPT TO BE)

Every workplace is going to have its ups and downs. But it is possible to find the positive elements or the humor in nearly any situation. Choose to be the person with the Chuck Norris jokes to lighten the mood of the self-deprecating humor to make those around you laugh at your expense. Remember, a spoonful of sugar makes the medicine go down.

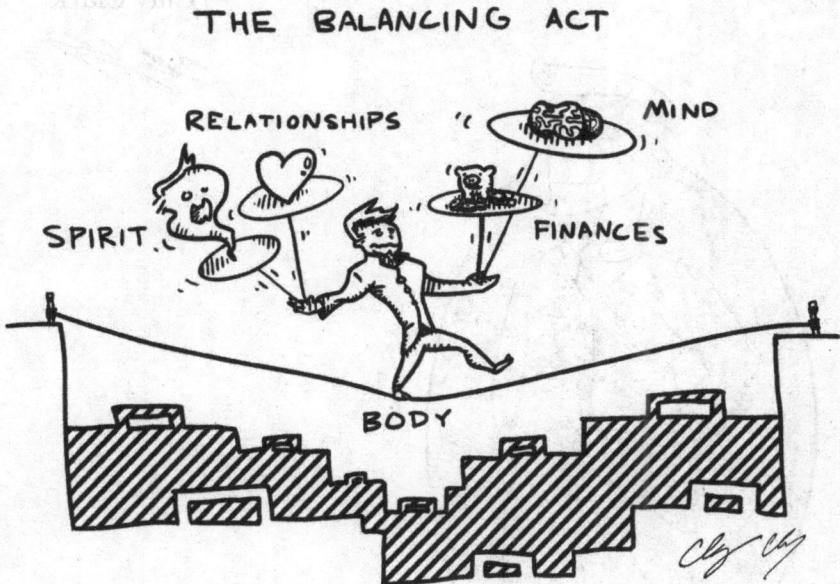

THE BALANCING ACT

ENTREPRENEURSHIP AT THE CORE INCLUDES FOUR STEPS:

» **Step 1** — Find a problem.

» **Step 2** — Solve the problem.

» **Step 3** — Sell the solution at a profit.

» **Step 4** — Nail it and scale it at a sustainable profit.

Once you master these four steps as an entrepreneur, you will become successful. Here's to your success!

— Clay Clark

IT'S NOT ABOUT HOW MUCH YOU MAKE,
ITS ABOUT HOW MUCH YOU KEEP.
-CLAY CLARK

CLAY CLARK'S BUSINESS COACHING EXPERIENCE (SINCE 2005)

★★★★★
EXPERIENCE THE WORLD'S HIGHEST RATED AND MOST REVIEWED BUSINESS CONFERENCE.

Reduce your marketing costs by 90% and save hundreds of hours and thousands of dollars!

As Seen On: Bloomberg BUSINESS INSIDER FAST COMPANY Forbes pandodaily

Service		Value	Price
Graphic Designers		$4,000 - $8,000 / month (compare to in-house designer and creativestate.com)	Included
Web Designers		$5,000 - $7,000 / month (compare to SEOInc.com, CreativeState.com, TheModStudio.com or GraphicGranola.com)	Included
Search Engine Optimization		$2,000 - $5,000 / month	Included
Proven Templates, Systems, & Examples		Save years of trial and error	Included
Executive Coaching		$5,000 - $10,000 value (compare with MauiMastermind.com & tonyrobbins.com)	Included
Public Relations Coaching		$2,000 - $10,000 / month (compare OKCNews.com and WallerPR.com)	Included
Online Advertisement / Reputation Management		$1,000 - $2,000 / month	Included
Sales Training		$4,000 - $5,000 / month (compare with GrantCardone.com and DaleCarnegie.com)	Included
Speaking Coaching		$2,500 / month	Included
Personal Finance Coaching		$1,000 / month	Included
Total		**$26,500 / month**	Month to Month Coaching

Average client growth rate of 104%. See client success stories at ThrivetimeShow.com

CLAY CLARK

"No one lives long enough to learn everything they need to learn starting from scratch. To be successful, we absolutely, positively have to find people who have already paid the price to learn the things we need to learn to achieve our goals."
— *Brian Tracy, Bestselling Author*

"See thouest a man diligent in his business? He shall stand before kings. He shall not stand before mean men."
— *Proverbs 22:19*

"Stop wasting thousands of dollars while chasing artisans, divas, videographers, web designers, photographers and drone pilots around."
— Clay Clark, Former US SBA Entrepreneur of the Year and Founder of Thrive15.com

Learn More at ThrivetimeShow.com

211

"The quality of a leader is reflected in the standards they set for themselves."

-Ray Kroc
(The man who franchised McDonald's and who bought the San Diego Padres in 1974)

"By default, 96% of businesses fail."
INC. MAGAZINE
https://www.inc.com/bill-carmody/why-96-of-businesses-fail-within-10-years.html

WHAT DOES A SUCCESSFUL BUSINESS SYSTEM LOOK LIKE?

① ESTABLISH REVENUE GOALS

What are your yearly gross revenue goals?
_____

What are your total weekly gross revenue goals?
_____

② DETERMINE THE BREAK-EVEN NUMBERS

Number of customers/sales to break even?
_____

③ DEFINE WORK WEEK: NUMBER OF HOURS

How many hours are you willing to work?
_____

What are your boundaries?
_____

⑥ CREATE 3-LEGGED MARKETING STOOL

Leg 1 _____

Leg 2 _____

Leg 3 _____

⑤ IMPROVE BRANDING

On a scale of 1-10, with 10 being the highest, how highly would you rate your website, print pieces, and social media?
_____

④ DEFINE YOUR UNIQUE VALUE PROPOSITION:

Who are your top 3 competitors?
_____

Have you mystery shopped your competitors?

⑤ CREATE A SALES CONVERSION SYSTEM

Sales scripts? _____
Recorded calls? _____
One sheets? _____
Pre-written emails? _____
Lead trackers? _____

⑥ DETERMINE SUSTAINABLE CUSTOMER ACQUISITION COSTS

What does it cost to obtain each customer?
_____

Do you have a tracking sheet? _____

Weekly advertising spend? _____

⑦ CREATE REPEATABLE SYSTEMS, PROCESSES, AND FILE ORGANIZATION

What daily, core, repeatable, actionable processes are not documented into script or checklist form? _____

What processes and systems are not repeatable?
_____

Do you have checklists for all positions?

⑩ CREATE HUMAN RESOURCES AND RECRUITMENT SYSTEMS

• Who are your A players? _____
• Who are your B players? _____
• Who are your C players? _____
• When is your weekly staff meeting? _____
• When is your weekly group interview? _____

⑨ CREATE A SUSTAINABLE AND REPETITIVE WEEKLY SCHEDULE

When is your weekly group interview? _____

When is your daily group huddle? _____

⑧ CREATE MANAGEMENT EXECUTION SYSTEMS

What people on your team will not do their jobs?
_____

Do you have merit-based pay installed? _____

⑪ CREATE YOUR ACCOUNTING AND AUTOMATE THE EARNING OF MILLIONS

Are you using Clay Clark's Ultimate tracking sheet? _____

⑫ DETERMINE THE POINT OF ACHIEVING FINANCIAL SUCCESS?

F7 GOALS
1·Faith _____
2·Family _____
3·Friendship _____
4·Fitness _____
5·Finances _____
6·Fun _____
7·Focus _____

SUPER MOVES FOR ENHANCING YOUR BRANDING

1. Create a website that is better than your competition.

2. Create a logo that is better than your competition.

3. Create a one sheet that clearly shows the value between you and the competition.

4. Create print materials that are better than your competition.

5. Create a marketing video that succinctly explains what problems you solve, who you are, and why people should buy from you.

6. Create signage that will wow your ideal and likely buyers.

7. Make sure that everything that your customers see or experience is first-class and intentional.

8. Create Google My Business account: business.google.com.

9. Get Google reviews.

10. Gather testimonial videos from your happy clients.

11. Have your team wear memorable uniforms.

12. Create a story video.

From the list below, circle which marketing vehicles that you think are most likely to carry your marketing message effectively to your ideal and likely buyers:

Adwords

Amazon.com

Automobile Wraps

Billboard Advertising

Blog Based Advertising

Business Development /
Partnership Deals

Buying Your Competition /
Mergers and Acquisition

Celebrity Endorsement

Cold Call Marketing

Door to Door Sales

Dream 100

Email Marketing

Facebook Advertising

Flyers

Google Maps

Google Reviews

Google Shopping

Magazine Advertising

Mall / Shopping Center
Traffic

Mass Mailers

Mass Texting (Twilio)

Mass Voicemails
(Slybroadcast)

Mass Emails (AWeber,
Constant Contact)

Networking Intentionally
(Set number of meetings
per month and specific
organizations)

Newspaper Advertising

Outdoor Signage

Pandora.com Radio
Advertising

Pay Per Click - Search
Engine Marketing /
Advertising

Pop-Up Shop

Public Relations
- Celebrity Tie-In Strategy
- Expert Strategy
- Giveback Strategy
- National News Tie-In
  Strategy
- Shock and Awe Strategy

Radio Advertising

Referral Based Advertising

Retargeting Online ads (See
SEO Conversion checklist)

Search Engine Optimization
(See next pages for details)

Sign-Based Marketing

Sign-Flipper Marketing

Social Media Advertising

Speech Based Marketing

Spotify Advertising

Targeted Online ads

Television Advertising

Text Marketing

Trade Show Advertising

Valpak Advertising

Yelp Reviews

YouTube Advertising

**Bias Alert...
But Still True**

ThriveTime Show
sponsors make
more money
than they spend
on advertising.

Taking the Limiters Off of Your Growth

Alright, now that we have determined what our ideal and likely buyers want, hopefully they are starting to buy our products and services from us often enough for us to be able to make a profit (although at this point, it's probably a small one). Now, it's time to teach you how to quickly identify and eliminate barriers, limiting beliefs, and systems that are causing your business to become stuck or to grow at a very slow annual growth rate. After working with thousands of companies, the Thrive15.com Mentors and I can all confidently say that you will never do this if you do not consistently schedule a specific time in your calendar to intentionally compare the direction your company is actually going versus the direction you had planned for the company to go.

> "Drifting, without aim or purpose, is the first cause of failure."
> -*Napoleon Hill*
> **(Bestselling author of** *Think & Grow Rich***)**

Schedule a weekly, one hour or 90-minute recurring meeting where you look at big wins of the week, the status of your team's key performance indicators, any big issues or burning fires that need to be solved, any low hanging fruit that your sales team needs to focus on, following up on the status of action items from last week and assigning action items for the following week. To help insure that your weekly meetings have a concrete and definitive agenda, we have provided the Perfect Weekly Meeting Agenda Template[64] at www. Thrive15.com/ThePerfectWeeklyMeetingAgendaTemplate.

The items to be covered during each Perfect Weekly Meeting include:

» Big wins of the week _____

» The vision of your company / why your business exists

_____

» What problems are your ideal and likely buyers willing to pay to solve?

_____

» The status of key performance indicators (quantifiable sales numbers and key performance metrics) _____

» Biggest limiting factors _____

» Burning fires _____

» Low hanging sales fruit _____

» Follow-up action items (did everyone get their assignments done?) _____

» Assign action items (who, what, when?) _____

Your commitment to follow this agenda each week will keep your company from ever drifting too far away from your core customers, your core vision, your core brand and your core values. However, there is much in the way of practical action steps that must be taken after these meetings if your company is going to succeed and truly grow quickly. First up is the area of HR... ahh... human resources. From my experience coaching companies all over the planet, I believe this is perhaps the single most challenging aspect of running a business, once you have figured out how to consistently produce and sell a product or service that the marketplace wants. Without quality and well-trained people in place, your business systems and visions will eventually die. However, do not get overwhelmed by the "BIG IDEA" of hiring people. To improve the quality of your life by 3%, I have broken up the entire human resources system into four segments:

1 Recruit

2 Hire

3 Inspire

4 Fire Those You Cannot Inspire and Who Cannot Do What Is Required

Step 1: Recruit

Let's start with the recruiting aspect of the business. You must view the human resources aspect of your business as the LIFEBLOOD OF YOUR BUSINESS. Without quality people, nothing will get done and thus, you must focus on recruiting. When I say focus, I mean to F.O.C.U.S. This stands for "focus on core tasks until success." My friend, you cannot ever take the pedal off of the metal when it comes to recruiting. So how do you do this? First off, you must create a winning job post that generates inquiries.[65] Nobody wants to work in a dead-end job with no career opportunities, no ongoing education, and no potential for benefits and bonuses, and no one wants to work in a negative or no-culture business for an absent and uninspiring boss. However, this is exactly what most job posts describe. If you are going to post a job opportunity on Craigslist, Monster, Indeed, or other third party source, you are going to be spending money to do so – don't waste it. Your job posts must be inspiring and must resonate with highly motivated people who are looking for a career and not just a job. Visit www.ThriveTimeShow.com/TreasureTrove to find a sample job post that is both practical and inspiring.

The statistics show us that most people hate or strongly dislike their jobs, so you must offer an alternative to these workplaces most people do not like.

✦ Mystic Statistic:

"Less than one-third (31.5%) of U.S. workers were engaged in their jobs in 2014."

Amy Adkins, author of "Majority of U.S. Employees Not Engaged Despite Gains in 2014," Gallup, January 28, 2015

Schedule a Time to Post Your Weekly Job Posts

If you do not schedule a specific time to post your job posts, you won't do it. You will get busy or you will forget. Do not let this happen to you. Block out time in your schedule right now for posting job opportunities. You must also determine what job posting boards or third-party sites you are going to post on. From my experience working with neurologists, dentists, photographers, limo drivers, and nearly every other industry under the sun, Craigslist is the most effective and lowest-cost platform on which to post your available jobs. However, I would strongly recommend that you post on Monster.com, Indeed.com and Craigslist.com simultaneously. I would budget for it and I would never stop.[67]

> "Kelleher believes that hiring employees who have the right attitude is so important that the hiring process takes on a "patina of spirituality." In addition, he believes that anyone who looks at things solely in terms of factors that can easily be quantified is missing the heart of business, which is people."
>
> *-Harvard Business Review Magazine (March-April 1994)*
> **(Putting the Service-Profit Chain to Work by James L. Heskett, Thomas O. Jones, Gary W. Loveman, W. Earl Sasser, Jr. and Leonard A. Schlesinger)**

Block Off Weekly Times for New Recruit Interviews

I'm busy and you're busy, but you and I must block off time to conduct weekly interviews to find people who will best represent our company. I love scheduling group interviews because it saves time and allows me to see how candidates compare with each other in a literal side-by-side comparison. A tryout of sorts. If you don't want to do group interviews, then you are going to have to block out many hours throughout your week to interview potential candidates who might or might not show up on time or at all for their interviews. Because

I realize that 40% of potential candidates don't have the mental capacity or the diligence needed to actually show up on time for their initial interviews, I love the group interview format. When someone responds to a job post, our team schedules them for an interview without even reading their resume first. We don't tell them the format of the interview - group or individual - we just tell them that we can interview them at this specific time on this specific date. To download an example of the email we send out to potential candidates to invite them for an interview, go to: www. ThriveTimeShow.com/TreasureTrove.

> "I don't know whether it was Calvin Coolidge or Bianca Jagger who said — they're both thin, that's why I get them confused — 'the business of business is business.' We've always said, 'The business of business is people.'"
>
>
>
> **-Herb Kelleher**
> **(The co-founder and former CEO of Southwest Airlines)**

Conduct Your Interviews with Both Passion and Purpose While Following an Agenda

During an interview, so many business owners spend massive quantities of time going on and on about their company and their vision while the candidates sit quietly, scanning the room for a blunt object with which they can respectfully bash in their skull to stop the boredom. Candidates begin to feel as though the person interviewing them has no game plan or agenda, because they don't. To make matters worse, most companies delegate the recruitment and interviewing process to "the new guy" or the person on your staff who hasn't quite found his place within your company culture. This is terrible.

My friend, the person conducting the interviews must look sharp and must be a confidence-inspiring powerhouse who can follow the perfect interview agenda every time; an agenda which includes:

» Clarifying the goals of the company

» Clarifying the goals of the candidate

» Clarifying the expectations of the job

» Clarify the compensation of the job

» Clarifying the career path of the job

» Answering any questions

» Clarifying the next steps for the applicants

To download the Perfect Interview Agenda, go to:
www.ThriveTimeShow/TreasureTrove.

To watch a training video on how to properly conduct a group interview, visit:
www.ThriveTimeShow/TreasureTrove.

What Are You Looking for in a Potential New Hire?

When you are interviewing candidates, you are looking for what the legendary CEO Jack Welch calls the "4 E's."

» **Energy** – Does the candidate have the energy to bring enthusiasm to the workplace every day?

» **Energize** – Does the candidate have the ability to energize those around him or her?

» **Edge** – Does the candidate have the edge needed to make the tough decisions?

» **Execute** – Does the candidate have the ability to execute and actually get their job done?

» **BONUS** – I have also found that it is extremely important that you search for candidates who are coachable.

"85% of job applicants lie on resumes."

-Inc. Magazine

Deep Thoughts:

Schedule Time for Candidates You Like to Shadow Your Team Before Calling References

If you like a few of the candidates you interviewed, that is great; however, statistics show that people you like may not impress you so much once they start doing the job. CBS News featured an article written by Rich Russakoff and Mary Goodman called "Employee Theft: Are You Blind to It?" This article revealed that the U.S. Chamber of Commerce estimates that 75% of employees steal from the workplace and that most do so repeatedly. CNBC also published a disturbing article written by Cindy Perman titled, "Employees Behaving Badly: Vampires and Gossips," stating that 43% of human resources managers said the number one reason a new employee didn't work out was because he or she couldn't accept feedback. My friend, the sad fact is that most people you interview will not work out. You want to find out who will not work out as soon as possible, before investing the time and money needed to pay for formal background checks and verify references.

Mystic Statistic

"The average cost of a bad hiring decision can equal 30% of the individual's first-year potential earnings."

US Department of Labor

The Shadowing Process Almost Always Confirms or Denies Job Candidates within the First Four Hours

Now I am going to explain how the shadowing process works. After you conduct enough group or individual interviews to lose a little faith in humanity, you may also have found a few people whom you believe might be the "perfect fit." The next step is to schedule them to shadow you or one of your top performers at the workplace. The candidate should be instructed to dress in appropriate work attire and act as if they already have the job. Explain to them that this process is designed so that both you and they can see if this opportunity is a great fit for you both.

> ## "75% of employees steal from the workplace and that must do so repeatedly."
>
> *-U.S. Chamber of Commerce*

During this shadowing process, approximately 50% of the candidates you initially liked will show themselves to be crazy, dishonest, drunk, or uncoachable. The other half will show themselves to be hireable. This is why we complete the shadowing process before checking references and investing in professional background checks.

Background Checks and References

Once you have found a candidate you really like, it is now time to conduct a professional background check and call their references. I can't explain to you how important this is. I recommend using GoodHire.com because they have low cost options, they have an easy-access online portal, and you can purchase one background check at a time. Visit www.GoodHire.com to check the backgrounds of potential candidates.

Mystic Statistic

"The U.S. Chamber of Commerce estimates that 75% of employees steal from the workplace and that most do so repeatedly."

"Employee Theft: Are You Blind to It?" – Rich Russakoff and Mary Goodman – CBSNews / MoneyWatch

☺ **Fun Fact:**

"78% of the men interviewed had cheated on their current partner."
The Washington Post

FAILURE TO DOCUMENT
LEADS TO PERPETUAL CONFUSION

DEEP THOUGHTS FROM THE MATTRESS KING

" "

Nothing works unless you do. The mattresses won't sell themselves.

— *Darren Conrad*

I sincerely believe that a business exists to create both time and financial freedom for the business owner by providing an incredible solution, product or service to the marketplace. However, as you grow your business you will soon discover that there will always be a never-ending conflict that you will experience on a daily basis that I refer to as the 3Ps.

» Pay - All employees want to be paid more.

» Price - All customers want to pay a lower price.

» Profits - Outside of Darren Conrad and I, very few people will care about the overall profitability of your business.

Thus, you must embrace the challenges that you will face on a daily basis as an entrepreneur because you know that these challenges are a prerequisite to the ultimate success that you desire. We believe in you. If you read this book, we know that you have both the mental capacity and the tenacity needed to turn your dreams into reality. So out there and seize the day. This is your year to Thrive if you choose to being the Big Ovewheleming Optimistic Momentum that it takes on a daily basis to overcome the obstacles that you are certain to face as an entrepreneur. We believe in you. Now go and make it happen! BOOM!

Sincerely,

Clay Clark

Co-host with Dr. Robert Zoellner of the ThriveTime Radio Show Podcast

Oklahoma 2007 U.S. SBA Entrepreneur of the Year, 2002 Tulsa Metro Chamber of Commerce Entrepreneuer of the Year, U.S. Chamber National Blue Ribbon Quality Award Winner, Blah, Blah, Blah, Etc.

Founder of DJConnection.com, EITRLounge.com, EpicPhotos.com, MakeYourLifeEpic.com, Thrive15.com Online Education, the ReAwaken America Tour

Co-Founder of 5 Kids (Read Fast Company Article for Proof)